Birds of the
Masai Mara

Adam Scott Kennedy

PRINCETON
press.princeton.edu

Published by Princeton University Press,
41 William Street, Princeton, New Jersey 08540
In the United Kingdom: Princeton University Press, 6 Oxford Street,
Woodstock, Oxfordshire OX20 1TW
nathist.press.princeton.edu

British Library Cataloging-in-Publication Data is available

Library of Congress Control Number 2012941171
ISBN 978-0-691-15594-4

Production and design by **WILD**Guides Ltd., Old Basing, Hampshire UK.
Printed in Singapore

10 9 8 7 6 5 4 3 2 1

Dedication

Dedicated to my parents, family and friends

Contents

BIRDS OF MARSH AND WATER

BIRDS OF WOODLAND, SCRUB & GARDEN

BIRDS OF ACACIA SCRUB

VILLAGE BIRDS

FOREST BIRDS

The mighty Mara River, with the Mara Triangle and the Oloololo Escarpment beyond.

About this book

The Masai Mara is world-famous for the spectacular Wildebeest migration that passes through each year but it is the incredible birdlife of the National Reserve that still astounds me to this day. When I arrived to manage Naibor Camp with my wife Vicki in February 2010, I was amazed to find that there was not a dedicated bird guide to this bird-rich reserve. Regional birding legend Brian Finch had created highly detailed checklists of the species he had logged while birding here over a 15-year period but even these were out of print and impossible to find.

The safari guides working with us at Naibor had a very good understanding of the birdlife, or *avifauna*, in the Mara but I was surprised to discover that they had not recorded Northern Black Flycatcher in the camp, a species I was seeing next to the dining mess almost every day. I took a series of photographic images of that species, as well as Fork-tailed Drongo and Slate-coloured Boubou, and set about describing how best to separate these three similar black birds in the field for the benefit of the guides. Unfortunately, these same guides never received my identification notes on these small black birds because I got a little carried away and ended up writing this book instead! However, if they turn to *page 122*, they'll see exactly what I was trying to explain all those months ago.

Whilst the original idea for this book was to help the guides that live and work in the Mara to extend their knowledge of the common birds they can see here on a regular basis, I soon realized that it would also be useful to anyone visiting the area. It is important, particularly for the guides, to know which species are found here and which are not. Relying on the larger texts to the East African region is simply not enough, as the maps in those books lack the local detail. The following example illustrates this point. While photographing some glorious Yellow-throated Longclaw (*page 59*) recently, I was asked by a passing guide, laden with Leopard-hungry guests, what I was watching. When I told him my subject was birds, he looked around, saw my quarry and yelled to his guests "Oh it's just a Golden Pipit, let's go". I almost choked. Golden Pipits are pretty, yellow birds, common on the eastern safari circuit around Tsavo and such places and they do indeed look similar to Longclaws – BUT they do not occur in the Masai Mara (though it could potentially arrive as a vagrant in future).

The Yellow-throated Longclaw is a common bird of open plains.

I very much hope that this book will help guides and everyone visiting the area in their understanding of what is here and what is not. For guides, "know your local patch" is the golden rule.

In this book I have tried my level best to avoid OTJ – ornithological techno-jargon. My wife Vicki was not a birder when I met her and, in polite company at least, will not confess to being one now. But her interest in birds has grown and she is now quite capable of identifying most of the species illustrated in this book. However, the minute I start pointing out greyish *supercilia*, spotted *median coverts* and ochre *rectrices* (all classic OTJ), she switches off. I firmly believe that it doesn't help to bore people about birds when they're starting out. By all means share the really interesting stuff and your own personal experiences but leave the OTJ for those who understand the language you're talking about. Seriously snobby birders may sneer at some of the simple terms I have used, but if Vicki and the guides can understand them, anyone can – and that's what this book is all about. For this reason, I have opted not to include a diagram of the feathers and body parts of a bird (definitely OTJ) as I hope that everyone using this book will know the difference between a head, a wing and a tail.

As you can probably tell by now, I have tried to keep this book as light-hearted as possible and there are several pieces of text that I hope will raise a smile. After all, the life of birds and the people who named them are fascinating and, believe it or not, quite entertaining too!

About the images

In collating the photos for this book, I have tried to capture and include the most suitable images to show the variations in sex, age and plumage throughout the year (for example, breeding and non-breeding plumages), both within the species and between the species. Where I have failed to capture the bird in a desired plumage or pose, the lovely people at **WILD***Guides* have very kindly liaised with Greg & Yvonne Dean and Andy & Gill Swash at WorldWildlifeImages.com and obtained the images required. For that I am very grateful to all concerned, as these photos complement the book beautifully. Thanks also to Vicki for letting me use some of her images, which are wonderful. All images not taken by me are fully credited on *page 167*.

A White-backed Vulture soars over the great migration of Wildebeest

How to use this book

When it comes to organising which species follows which, most field guides follow a standard order, or systematic list. For this reason, in Africa at least, the Ostrich is first and buntings are last. For seasoned birders, this is great because we can pick up almost any bird guide and know that birds of prey (raptors) are quarter the way through, pigeons are somewhere in the middle, and finches are near the back. For those not so familiar with this order, it may require a dip into the index. But if you're not sure what species you're looking for, only that it is a finch of some kind, that's not much help. So this book, which is aimed at all levels of birding ability, adopts a habitat-based approach. Put simply, first decide where you are watching the bird, and then decide from the offering in that section which species you are most likely to be looking at. If you are on the plains and you see a large streaky lark with chestnut in its wings, check out the plains section and there you'll find it – a Rufous-naped Lark. If you are in the leafy gardens of your camp or lodge and you see a bright yellow and green bird, quite small and resembling a hummingbird at times, check out the woodland and gardens section and, low and behold, there it is – Collared Sunbird. I hope you find this as simple as it is intended to be.

Of course, birds are very mobile creatures that move around from one place to another – so there is every chance that you may encounter a species away from its typical habitat. Birds such as swallows and swifts spend much of their lives in the air and may not be restricted to any particular habitat. For that reason, such species have their own 'habitat' – up in the air – but guidance is still given about where you are most likely to find them. Similarly, nocturnal birds hide very well during the daytime and are most likely to be seen on tracks and roads at night, so a section for nocturnal birds was also required.

The English names used for the birds in this book are those adopted by the Bird Committee of Nature Kenya. As these may differ from the names given in other books, the most frequently used alternative English names are also referenced. A list of the universally recognized scientific names is included on *pages 168–170*. The sizes shown for each bird indicates their length from the tip of the bill to the end of the tail and are given in both centimetres (cm) and inches (").

To help keep a record of the birds you see in the Mara, a small tick-box has been included next to each species description. However, if you'd prefer not to 'spoil' your book, a checklist of the birds included can be downloaded from the **WILD***Guides* website www.wildguides.co.uk.

The stunning Collared Sunbird is common among the wooded gardens of camps and lodges.

The habitats

Nature does not permit easy categorization, and deciding which species fits into each habitat is not always straightforward. For example, in the middle of a vast grassy plain you may find a single thick bush with a bird sitting on top. Which habitat section of this book would you open to find and identify your mystery bird? The best place to start would be the **Plains** section – but if that fails, try the **Open woodland, bush and garden** section. However, if your bird has long legs and a strong bill that might be used for fishing, then maybe it's a species of heron that has made a quick pit-stop before flying on to the nearest marsh. In this case, you should find it in the **Marsh and water** section. Similarly, if you see a bird but you're not sure what it is, do try the quick key on the inside back cover.

The habitat sections in this book have been colour-coded in an attempt to make the process of finding your bird as simple as possible.

Plains	26–63
Marsh and water	64–91
Woodland, scrub and garden	92–143
Acacia scrub	144–149
Village	150–153
Forest	154–157
Up in the air	158–163
Nightbirds	164–165

Plains

The grassy plains cover the majority of land in the Mara and can be divided into two main types: short and long.

The short grass plains are continually grazed by the game and, in the conservancy lands, also by domestic animals. They provide limited protection for the birds that live there but do allow these species to see danger coming from afar.

Common species include various plovers and the smart **Temminck's Courser** (*page 32*).

The long grass plains consist of grass species that are not particularly palatable to grazing animals. These areas afford protective cover for ground-nesting birds such as the various **bustards** (*pages 30–31*), **longclaws** (*pages 58–59*) and **larks** (*pages 56–57*). Other species, including the **Buffy Pipit** (*page 58*), prefer to feed on the open short grass plain but nest in the longer grass.

Kori Bustard displaying

Red-capped Lark

15

Marsh and water

The Mara River is the most significant water body in the reserve but various smaller rivers (*e.g.* Talek) and streams (*e.g.* Olare Orok) flow into it. There are also some impressive marshes (*e.g.* Musiara), ox-bow lakes (many in the Mara Triangle) and permanent pools (*e.g.* at Keekorok Lodge).

After any substantial rainfall, many grassland areas of the reserve become waterlogged and afford feeding grounds for many typically wetland bird species such as **Hamerkop** (*page 76*) and **Three-banded Plover** (*page 84*).

Malachite Kingfisher

Three-banded Plover

Saddle-billed Stork

Woodland, scrub & garden

Many camps and lodges are located amongst tall trees which afford some protection from the sun's heat during the middle of the day. Camps such as Naibor, Rekero and Governors' are situated among riverine (or *riparian*) woodland, while others such as Sarova have a different array of tree species in their impressive gardens.

Several of the larger lodges, such as Keekorok, even have wonderfully manicured gardens with exuberant flowers and lawns, all of which offer superb feeding and breeding sites for a wide array of species not likely to be encountered elsewhere.

An early morning walk, starting around 6.30 am, around the camp or lodge where you are staying, preferably with a guide or bird enthusiast resident at the site, is highly recommended.

Klaas's Cuckoo

White-browed Robin Chat

Acacia scrub

A quintessentially *African* tree family, acacias are a varied mix of hardy trees and bushes that support a unique selection of birds. Although you may see scattered acacia trees almost anywhere in the reserve, the best acacia scrub habitats are found in the north and east of the reserve, primarily on conservancy lands.

Many of the special acacia bird species, such as **Silverbird** (*page 147*) and **Abyssinian Scimitarbill** (*page 144*) cover vast areas in a day – so expect to spend some time searching for them.

Vitelline Masked Weaver

Village

As with every other human habitation around the world, the Maasai towns and villages around the reserve are home to some resourceful species that have adapted successfully to a world created by people.

Crows (*page 153*) and several species of **sparrow** (*pages 150–151*) and **finch** (*page 152*) are most easily found around these places and many will be common close to some larger camps and lodges too.

Red-cheeked Cordon-bleu

Forest

Pages 154–157

The mature forest surrounding Kichwa Tembo/
Bateleur Camp in the north-west of the Mara is
the largest fragment of mature forest found in
the area and supports a number of special birds
that are rarely found elsewhere. In particular, the
huge fruiting fig trees are the main attraction to a
large forest **hornbill**, (*page 157*) colourful **turacos**
(*pages 154–155*) and **barbets** (*page 156*), not to
mention a selection of small unobtrusive birds.

Schalow's Turaco

Narina Trogon

Many birds can be seen flying from one place to another but there are two families of bird that spend most of their lives 'up in the air': the **swallows and martins** (*pages 158–161*) and the **swifts** (*pages 162–163*). Because they can cover such large areas in the course of the day, these birds are likely to be encountered over many different habitats – but their true habitat is the sky where they feed and, in the case of swifts, even mate on the wing.

Night birds

Owls and **nightjars** are birds of the night and although you may be fortunate enough to see them during the day, usually roosting but sometimes active, your best chance of an encounter is during a night-drive.

The rules of the Mara Reserve do not permit night-drives but if you are staying within one of the conservancies then a night-drive (highly recommended for birds and other animals) might be permitted, so do enquire with the staff.

Verreaux's Eagle Owl

The Gabon Nightjar is frequently encountered on roads and tracks at night.

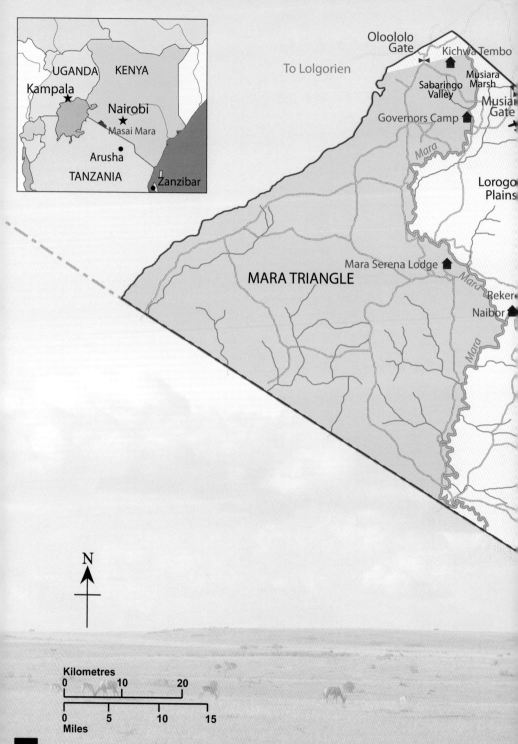

UGANDA KENYA

Kampala

Nairobi

Masai Mara

Arusha

TANZANIA   Zanzibar

Oloololo
Gate   Kichwa Tembo

To Lolgorien   Musiara
                          Sabaringo   Marsh
                          Valley   Musia
                                              Gate
            Governors Camp

                          Mara   Lorogo
                                                  Plains

                   Mara Serena Lodge

MARA TRIANGLE   Mara   Reker

                                              Naibor

N

Kilometres
0   10   20

0   5   10   15
Miles

Map of the Masai Mara
showing locations mentioned in the text

To Lemek

Olare Orok

Ol Kiombo airstrip

Talek

Talek Gate

Burrungat Plains

Talek

To Narok and Nairobi

Sekenani Gate

Sarova

Meta Plains

okout Hill

Keekorok

Olomutatiek Gate

Sand

Sand River Gate

Sand

TANZANIA

KENYA

25

■ Ostrich 250 cm 98″

Huge, unmistakable birds. Males are distinguished by their black body feathers, white wing plumes and short, white tail. The pink skin of the head, neck and long, strong legs becomes flushed when birds are excited. This is particularly so in display, which involves exuberant rolling and shaking of the wing plumes. Females and immature birds are greyish-brown in colour and lack pink tones to the skin. Eggs are laid in a scrape in the ground that several females may share. The call is a deep "*hoo-hoo-whooooooo*" that sounds similar to a Lion's roar from a distance.

RECORD BREAKER
This is the largest bird in the world, lays the largest and heaviest eggs, and is the only flightless bird of mainland Africa. Although it is the only bird in the world with two toes on each foot, the Ostrich is capable of sprints in excess of 60 kph, making it the fastest-running of all birds.

Chicks are able to walk within minutes of hatching and show a number of dark stripes on a rusty-coloured head and neck.

Secretarybird 140 cm 55″

A tall and elegant bird often seen walking through long grass in search of prey. Even from a considerable distance, the light-grey plumage with black flight feathers and knee-length 'trousers' is distinctive. The attractive face of bare, red skin is decorative, and there are black plumes at the back of the head. The sexes are alike. Immature birds are browner all-over with yellowish facial skin. The legs are long and pink and the toes are short. These it uses to club and tackle dangerous snakes, such as puff adder and cobra, although they will also take other reptiles, small birds and mammals. Birds typically roost on top of a solitary tree or bush, and it is in such places that they usually build their nest. In flight, the long, black-tipped, grey tail is conspicuous and it also shows a white rump. It is generally silent but sometimes growls, especially at the nest.

Although the head plumes may resemble a secretary's quill, the bird's name is actually a corruption of *saqr-et-tair*, an Arabic-based word meaning hunter-bird.

Grey Crowned Crane
110 cm 43″

Very attractive birds of open plains and marshes. The crown of fine, golden feathers sits on a black, velvety forehead, and below the clean white face disc hangs a red wattle. Although sometimes seen in large flocks, these birds are more often encountered in pairs walking sedately and feeding by pecking at seeds. If very lucky, you may see them break into a joyous, hopping display dance, which is one of the finest sights of the Mara. Pairs build a floating nest in a shallow pool. The chicks are yellow and rather cute, though immature birds are quite scruffy. The call is a loud honking "*hu-wonk*" that is often given in flight, when they also show large white patches on the forewing.

This is the national bird of Uganda, and is 'Grey' and 'Crowned' rather than 'Grey-crowned'. The distinction is made because there is also a Black Crowned Crane found in West Africa.

Black-bellied Bustard

White-bellied Bustard

■ Kori Bustard 128 cm 50″

A very large, thickset bird of open areas that often seeks shade under a tall tree. Males are considerably larger than females but the sexes are otherwise similar. The face, neck and breast are lightly barred with grey, the crown is black and there is a black stripe running through the eye. The back and flight feathers are greyish-brown and the upperwing is peppered with black and white markings. During their display (see *page 15*), which can be seen from a great distance, male birds will stand and strut with raised crest, the neck feathers puffed up into a large white balloon, and the tail brought up and over the back. The call is a deep repeated "*woomp*" given when in display.

RECORD BREAKER
The Kori Bustard can leap into flight from a standing start and is the heaviest of all flying birds, reaching 42 lb (19 kg).

Black-bellied Bustard 64 cm 25″

A small bustard of long grassy plains. During the breeding season (March to May), males perform an amazing display, usually from raised ground such as a grassy knoll. They stand with their neck raised then throw back their head abruptly making a "*kwaark*" sound. With the neck coiled back, the bird then growls softly before letting out the air in a belched "*pop!*" about five seconds after the initial recoil. On a quiet day, it is possible to hear other males making the same display call just a short distance away. Adult birds look spectacular in flight and show a strongly contrasting black-and-white wing pattern which is obvious from many kilometres away, especially as the males make exaggerated wing flaps during aerial circuits of their territories.

White-bellied Bustard 61 cm 24″

A small, pale bustard of short grassy areas, often with scattered small trees and shrubs. The black-and-white face markings of the male, finished with red 'lipstick' on the bill, are distinctive. When displaying to females, they walk with their neck outstretched and their black throat inflated. Females are similar to the female Black-bellied Bustard but can easily be separated by their stronger face markings and soft-blue colouration to the back of the neck. In flight, this species does not show any white in the wing. However, as with all bustards, it is reluctant to fly, preferring to walk away from danger instead.

Female

Male

Female

Male

■ Temminck's Courser 21 cm 8¼"

Small, erect-standing birds of the short grass plains. Usually found in pairs or small parties in very open areas, where they habitually run, stop and then peck at an item on the ground – often a small grub or other invertebrate. It is quite common to find them rummaging through a small dung pile, where various food items can be found. They are reluctant to fly, preferring to run from any threat, but when they do take flight they show a short tail, beyond which the long legs project, and very rounded wings that are entirely black underneath. This creates quite a distinctive silhouette. Four species of courser have been recorded in the Mara but this is by far the easiest to find as the others are primarily nocturnal.

Spur-winged Plover
(*page 82*)

Crowned Plover

Black-winged Plover

Temminck's Courser

Named after the Dutch explorer Coenraad Jacob Temminck (1778–1858) or maybe his father, both of whom were avid bird collectors.

Crowned Plover 31 cm 12¼"

Common and distinctive waders of open plains. This species is slightly larger than the Black-winged Plover and has longer, bright-pink legs. It is best identified by the characteristic head pattern (a black-and-white skullcap) from which it derives its name. This species also shows a unique wing pattern which makes it easy to separate from other large plovers, either in flight or when wing-stretching – something it often does when a vehicle approaches close-by. These birds draw a great deal of attention to themselves when performing noisy intimidation flights aimed at distracting predators, such as jackals, birds of prey and Southern Ground Hornbills (*page 35*), from their eggs or chicks. If the predator persists, the plovers will often resort to dive-bombing their enemies which can bring them perilously close to danger – so it is always worth watching to see who wins.

Black-winged Plover
27 cm 10½"

Chunky waders of open plains. Similar in shape and build to other large plovers (see also *pages 82,83,85*) but the only one that shows a clear black band across the breast. They are mostly blue-grey in the face and usually show a white spot above the bill, though this is less obvious in females. In flight, they show a distinctive wing pattern that separates it from other plovers. Black-winged Plovers are often found in loose flocks of up to 20 birds but during September to November they congregate in larger flocks, sometimes of more than 150 birds, especially in the north of the reserve. Their distinctive "*chi-chi-chi chireeek*" call can often be heard at night.

Large plovers within the scientific genus *Vanellus*, including those on this page and *pages 82–83*, are also known as lapwings.

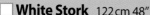 White Stork 122 cm 48″

Distinctive pied storks of long grass plains.
These birds are non-breeding migrants from Europe
that usually arrive into the Mara during October
and leave in late April, although a few birds have
been known to stay in southern Africa to breed.
Depending on the rains, many birds will
disperse into the Serengeti where they can be
seen feeding alongside the hordes of Wildebeest.
They frequently gather in vast flocks numbering
in excess of 5,000 birds. The only other 'white'
stork with which this bird could be confused
is the Yellow-billed Stork (*page 65*), but the
longer, yellow bill and red facial skin of that
species are distinctive. In Europe, White Storks
are frequently found nesting on the rooftops
of buildings and feature in traditional
European folklore as the
deliverer of babies.

As with all storks, the
White Stork has no
syrinx, or vocal cord,
which prohibits them
from making any
calls. Instead, you may
sometimes hear them
clatter their bills.

Abdim's Stork 81 cm 32"

A mostly black stork with a colourful face. Like the White Stork (*left*), the Abdim's Stork is a non-breeding migrant that arrives in vast numbers into the Mara. However, this bird is a migrant that breeds in central Africa where it is considered a good luck symbol and bringer of the rains. Like other grassland storks, this bird walks endlessly in search of grasshoppers, locusts, small reptiles and amphibians. Abdim's is the smallest of all true storks and shows a white belly in flight as well as a conspicuous white rump. This separates it from the rarely encountered Black Stork, another migrant from Europe, that has a black rump. ▼

Named after the Governor of Wadi Halfa, Ben El-Arnaut Abdim, a Turkish civil servant working in Sudan from 1821 to 1827, who assisted Rüppell (of Rüppell's Vulture fame, *page 37*) during his collecting expeditions in North Africa.

Southern Ground Hornbill
102 cm 40"

Huge, black, turkey-like terrestrial birds of the open plains. Usually encountered in family groups that may include immature birds and mature offspring of previous broods. Adults of both sexes show red facial skin and a saggy wattle, but the female can be separated by the small patch of violet-blue colour on the throat. Look out for the incredibly long eyelashes on this bird. They are reluctant fliers and prefer to hop and run away from danger but they will always fly to roost in trees at dusk when they reveal clean white outer flight feathers. Listen out for their wonderful calls, usually at dawn, a deep, booming *"ooomp-ooomp-wa-woomp"* that carries for many kilometres. ▼

Can walk for over 30 km a day in search of invertebrates, reptiles and young birds.

35

☐ Marabou Stork 152 cm 60″

A huge, ugly stork. This bird is a regular scavenger at the carcass where it uses its enormous bill to great effect. It will often wait for the more aggressive vultures to have their fill before stepping in to clean up the scraps. The head is mostly featherless which enables it to get deep into the carcass without getting blood over its plumage; bare skin being easier to keep clean than feathers. It is often found along the Mara River during the Wildebeest migration where it gathers in large numbers to feast on the many carcasses that litter the channels. Unlike other storks which fly with their necks outstretched, the Marabou carries its head against its body like a heron.

RECORD BREAKER
Some large individuals have a wingspan in excess of 3·5m (10 feet), making this species, together with the Andean Condor of South America, the longest-winged of all land birds.

In many parts of Africa, the Marabou is known as the 'undertaker' on account of its habit of opening its wings over a carcass as though it is measuring it up for a coffin!

Rüppell's Vulture 104 cm 41″

A larger vulture than the similar White-backed Vulture, Rüppell's is reliably told from that species by its cream-coloured bill at all ages. Adult birds also show obvious pale scalloping to the wing feathers and never a white rump in flight. Numbers of Rüppell's increase dramatically with the arrival of the Wildebeest migration but it can be found in the Mara year-round. It nests on remote, precipitous cliffs and therefore has to fly farther than the resident White-backeds. Being larger than the White-backed Vulture, it can easily use its strength to out-compete that species when similar numbers are present at the carcass, but it is rarely the first to arrive. ▼

This bird is named after the German Wilheim Rüppell (1794–1884) whose zoological and ethnographical collections from North Africa dated between 1822 and 1833.

White-backed Vulture 98 cm 39″

The commonest vulture in the Mara. At first glance, many vulture species may appear quite similar but it pays to know 'who is who' when watching these birds at the carcass as the different species have different feeding behaviours and strategies. White-backs play the 'numbers game', benefitting most when ten or more of its kind are at a carcass, and use intimidation tactics to push other, larger species away. It can be identified by the all-black bill (compare with Rüppell's Vulture) and the plain-brown plumage on the wings. Adult birds appear very pale, almost white, especially in flight when the belly and underwing contrast with the dark flight feathers. The white rump can only be seen from above and rarely when the bird is on the ground. Immature birds are mostly brown all-over, including the rump, but share the black bill of the adult. It is a regular breeder in the Mara, preferring to nest in trees, and affords some level of ▼ protection to other birds, such as starlings and weavers, that will nest in the same tree.

See *pages 40–41* for vultures in flight

◻ White-headed Vulture   84 cm 33″ ▶

An attractive-looking vulture with a pale head. This bird is the anomaly among vultures in that it rarely attends a large carcass. Instead, it prefers to seek out its own smaller prey items, although it will sometimes scavenge from a recent Bateleur or Tawny Eagle kill. Immature birds, which lack the crisp white head feathers of the adults, may struggle to find their own prey once they leave the nest and are more likely to visit a large carcass. However, because its strategy is simply to wait until the other large vultures have had their fill, it is often the last to feed alongside the smaller but more numerous Hooded Vultures. For this reason, White-headed Vultures are most likely to be encountered in flight, as they typically spend more hours searching for their prey. Adults of both sexes have a white belly and females have white in the flight feathers closest to the body. Immature birds in flight appear very dark, apart from the head, and may show a narrow white line cutting across the underwing from body to wing-tip. Just a few pairs nest in the Mara.

◻ Hooded Vulture   75 cm 30″

A small vulture with a bare pink head. Usually found in small groups, the Hooded Vulture is the smallest of the resident vultures in the Mara and is usually found at the periphery of the carcass waiting for the other, larger vultures to have their fill. Its bill is especially slim for a vulture as it does not need to rip open any skin or flesh; that work has already been done by the time it gets a chance to feed. Instead, it has the perfect tool for tearing at the smaller tendons and scraps often deep inside the remains of the carcass. Adult birds have a pink, bare-skinned face often topped with a 'woolly' wig. Immature birds show darker 'woolly' head feathers and blue skin on the face. In flight, it appears all-dark and the tail is short. Like the White-backed (*page 37*) and Lappet-faced Vultures, this bird nests in trees, although very few pairs breed locally.

Immature
Hooded Vulture

Immature
White-headed Vulture

Adult
Hooded
Vulture

Adult
White-headed
Vulture

■ **Lappet-faced Vulture** 115 cm 45″

The king of the African vultures. Its huge ivory-coloured bill and overall size make the Lappet-faced Vulture a very impressive sight at any carcass, although the saggy, bare-skinned face tends to make it look rather unattractive. In flight, the vast, broad wings show a clear white line across the 'arm' and the white 'leggings' can give it a white-bellied appearance. The tail is short and obviously wedge-shaped. Immature birds are similar but the face is often less pink and it lacks the white leggings of the adult, which become more obvious as the bird reaches maturity at around six years of age. Although this species is far less numerous than the White-backed and Rüppell's Vultures (*page 37*), its feeding strategy is simple and successful – sheer size and power – and it will dominate over any number of other vultures at the carcass. It breeds at low densities in the Mara, usually nesting in the top of an acacia or desert palm tree.

Adult
Lappet-faced
Vulture

See *pages 40–41* for vultures in flight

■ **Hooded Vulture** (*page 38*) ▶
Wingspan 170 cm 67"

The 'small' one (but still a very
large bird). The darkest of the vultures,
though adults show a silvery sheen to
the base of their flight feathers.

■ **Lappet-faced Vulture** (*page 39*)
Wingspan 290 cm 114"

The 'massive' one.
An enormous bird with baggy white
'shorts' and an obvious white bar
across the front of the underwing.
The large, pink head is usually visible.
▼

◀ ■ **Rüppell's Vulture**
(*page 37*)
Wingspan 260 cm 102"

The 'scaly' one.
Look out for cream
bars running across
the belly and
underwing.

Vultures in flight
Identifying vultures in flight can be straightforward if you know what you're looking for...

■ White-headed Vulture (*page 38*) ▶
Wingspan 215 cm 85″

The 'easy' one. Extensive white on the belly and, in females, white inner flight feathers are give-aways.

Immature

◀ **■ White-backed Vulture**
(*page 37*)
Wingspan 230 cm 90″

The 'common' one. Adult have a white underwing contrasting with the darker flight feathers. Immatures are dark-brown under much of the wing and show a white bar near the front of the wing.

Adult

Martial Eagle 84 cm 33"

A massive, powerful eagle of open areas. The greyish-brown
head, back and chest of the adult contrasts with the
white belly that always shows large, dark spots. Young birds
(*page 46*) are much whiter and lack the all-dark head.
In flight, the underwing appears very dark. Birds are often
seen soaring high in search of prey but will also watch for
prey from a perch. This is a ferocious predator that
is known to kill baboons, antelope and large birds
including storks, guineafowl and even other birds
of prey. It usually nests on top of a large tree.

■ Bateleur 70 cm 28″ ▶

The classic soaring bird of the open plain. It shows a distinctive silhouette in flight (*page 47*) with swept-back, angular wings and a tail so short that it sometimes appears to have no tail at all. The black, cigar-shaped body and chestnut tail of the adult contrasts markedly with the white underwing, which always shows a black edge to the rear (this is narrow in males and broad in females). Females also show a large, grey band in the flight feathers that can be seen on the upperwing in flight and when perched. Both sexes have red legs and a bare, red face, while immatures show blue-green bare parts and a uniform brown plumage. The commonly heard call is a gruff "*yaaargh*", which is often followed by rapid flapping of the wings. Prey items include small mammals, reptiles and birds, and it is also an active scavenger.

Bateleur is the French word for acrobat and was given to the bird on account of its habit of tipping for balance in flight like a tight-rope walker.

◀ ■ Black-chested Snake Eagle 68 cm 27″

A medium-sized, black-and-white eagle of the open plains. It appears similar to the much larger Martial Eagle but adults show a darker head and lack the spots on the belly. In flight (*page 46*), the underwing appears mostly white with three or four narrow black bars running across the flight feathers. Immature birds are mostly brown with a pale face and the underparts are mottled with untidy rufous patches. Snake eagles lack the baggy, feathered thighs of Martial Eagle and show bare, grey legs when perched. It will sometimes use an exposed perch to watch for its next meal – but look out for this bird hovering in search of snakes and other reptiles.

☐ **Black Kite** 61 cm 24″ ▶

An all-dark raptor with a distinctive silhouette in flight (*page 47*): the long wings are typically held with a strong angle at the bend, and it usually shows a noticeable fork in its long tail. In both adult and immature birds, much of the plumage is uniform dark-brown. It can be told from eagles by the smaller, yellow bill. The Black Kite has a wide distribution across Europe, Africa and Asia, and some ornithologists consider our resident birds to be a distinct species, known as Yellow-billed Kite.

This is a classic scavenger of urban areas that is common in big cities and small villages, although it can sometimes be seen at carcasses with the much larger vultures.

Look out for this bird perched on telegraph poles and roadside posts, when it can be very approachable.

◀ ☐ **Augur Buzzard** 60 cm 24″

A broad-winged raptor of arid areas. Two distinct colour variations are found in the Mara, known as light and dark forms, although the light form is by far the most common. Light birds show an all-white throat, breast and belly, whereas dark birds are mostly black all-over. In flight (*page 46*), all birds show white at the base of the flight feathers, and a view of the upperwing reveals a chequered pattern on these same feathers. All adults show a rich-orange tail, though the tail is brown in immature birds. They frequently hover for long periods or just hang in the wind barely moving their wings. This is the only resident buzzard in the Mara and is most often found in the dry areas to the north and east of the reserve.

44

☐ Tawny Eagle 74 cm 29″

The common large, brown eagle of open plains. Tawny Eagles are highly variable in their colouration, with some birds being pale-cream and others very dark with rich chestnut tones, but most are a light coffee-brown. When perched they show a bright yellow gape extending from the strong, hooked bill, and well-feathered legs. Immatures tend to be paler and show whitish lines through the wing that are obvious in flight. As with many birds of prey, Tawny Eagles are most often encountered in flight (*page 47*), when they appear large and robust and show mostly dark flight feathers and a dark tail. It is quite common to see these resident eagles moulting, with wing and tail feathers either missing or still growing, which can give them a scruffy-looking appearance. They are very active hunters of small mammals, such as hares, mongooses and dik-diks, as well as gamebirds and large reptiles including monitor lizards. However, this does not put them above scavenging and they will often flush smaller raptors off their kill and attend a carcass with vultures, where their barking or growling calls are most often heard.

■ Augur Buzzard ▶
(*page 44*)
Wingspan 137 cm 54″

A round-winged
raptor with a short,
reddish tail.

Dark form

Light form

Immature

Adult

◀ ■ Martial Eagle
(*page 42*)
Wingspan 260 cm 102″

A massive eagle.
Adults show a dark head
and underwing, while
immatures are
mostly pale beneath
with light barring
on the tail and
flight feathers.

■ Black-chested Snake Eagle ▲
(*page 43*) Wingspan 175 cm 69″
Like a small Martial Eagle but much paler
underneath. The underwing is especially
white, with a few narrow bars along the flight
feathers only. It lacks black spots on the belly
but shows a strongly barred tail.

Adult

Immature

◀ ■ **Bateleur** (*page 43*)
Wingspan 175 cm 69"

The uniquely shaped
'bulging' wings are often
swept-back and the red tail
is very short. Immatures
begin very brown all-over
but become increasingly
mottled with black
as they mature.

■ **Black Kite** (*page 44*)
Wingspan 150 cm 59"

An all-brown raptor with
a distinctive fork in the tail.

▼

Flying raptors
These can be
challenging but
always try to
make an educated
guess using the
following hints.

■ **Tawny Eagle** (*page 45*) ▶
Wingspan 190 cm 75"

A large brown eagle with a broad,
rounded tail.

47

▲
☐ **African Harrier Hawk** 66 cm 26″

An elegant grey raptor with a bare face. Adult birds are mostly grey with white, finely barred underparts. In flight, the long black tail shows a single white band and the wings are grey and broad with darker flight feathers. The bare facial skin is yellow but this often flushes to bright pink when the bird becomes excited. Immature birds are mostly brown and nondescript. Food items include palm fruits and a variety of reptiles and young birds. Unique among African raptors, the Harrier Hawk has double-jointed legs which enable it to explore nest holes of birds by rotating the talons all the way around. Look out for it flying along the edge of the plain and resting in exposed trees where weavers are nesting. It is commonly known as the Gymnogene in southern Africa.

Montagu's Harrier is Named after Colonel George Montagu (1751–1815), a keen British naturalist and soldier who served in the American Revolution who, unfortunately, died of tetanus after stepping on a rusty nail.

Male

Male

Montagu's Harrier

Female

☐ Montagu's Harrier 46 cm 18″

A graceful long-winged bird of open grasslands. The sexes are very different in appearance, with males mostly grey and females streaky brown. Immature birds are similar to females but show a dark face patch and warm-orange colouration to the underparts and underwing. In the buoyant flight, males show black tips to the wing and a narrow black bar along the middle of the upperwing. The brown females show a whitish belly streaked with brown and a clean white rump patch. Females and immatures of this and similar harrier species are commonly known as 'ringtails'. The similar Pallid Harrier (*not shown*) also occurs in the Mara but can be difficult to separate. Montagu's Harrier is a long-distance migrant from Europe and Asia and can usually be found between October and May. Birds often gather to roost, particularly on airstrips.

☐ African Black-shouldered Kite

35 cm 14″

A small, pale raptor of open areas, often encountered perched on top of an acacia. It appears white below and grey above, with a dark patch on each 'shoulder'. A close view will reveal bright-red eyes. When perched, notice how the long wings extend beyond the very short, white tail. When searching for prey, such as grasshoppers and small reptiles, it will circle an area of grassland and hover frequently, when it could be mistaken for a kestrel (*pages 50–51*) – although these falcons have a much longer tail. It has recently become known as the Black-winged Kite, but for ease of reference the old familiar name is used here.

49

Grey Kestrel 33 cm 13″

A stocky, all-grey kestrel.
Often found perched in a bare
tree, especially along the lower
reaches of the Mara River,
where it watches patiently for
a variety of prey, including
grasshoppers and termites.
Its bare parts are bright-yellow
and contrast markedly with the
slate-grey plumage. In flight,
look out for the finely barred
tail and the chequered pattern
on the flight feathers. It lays its
eggs in the old nests of other
birds, with a preference for
those of the Hamerkop.

▶

Lanner Falcon 46 cm 18″

A large, powerful falcon of open areas.
The broad, pointed wings and chunky tail
are perfectly designed for aerial combat.
Watching a Lanner chase its prey, usually a
bird up to the size of a small bustard, in
mid-air can be just as exciting as a Cheetah
in full chase. Sometimes they will attempt to
tackle even larger prey, such as small antelope
and monkeys, but this is quite unusual.
They appear very pale from below and
slate-grey from above. A good view may
also reveal a smart black moustache and
a chestnut patch on the back of the neck.
Immature birds are much browner and show
a heavily spotted belly and dark underwing.
The Lanner is usually solitary but sometimes
flies in family groups, when adults teach
young birds the skills they require.

▼

Lanner Falcon

Grey Kestrel

Common Kestrel

■ **Common Kestrel** 33 cm 13"
A brown-backed falcon with a long tail. Found in singles and groups, these kestrels are frequently seen hovering over the grass in search of small prey before diving steeply onto their quarry. The sexes are fairly similar although males show more grey in the head and tail; young birds are mostly brown. In flight, all birds show a dark band at the end of the tail. Resident birds, sometimes known as 'Rock Kestrels', are supplemented by migratory birds from Europe and Asia between October and April. Birds often come together to roost on the top of an acacia or desert palm tree, when you may hear their excited high-pitched calls "*kee-kee-kee*".

Male

Female

☐ Yellow-throated Sandgrouse 31 cm 12¼"

A gregarious, stocky bird of the very short grass plains. In their rapid, direct flight these birds can be mistaken for overweight pigeons; on the ground they behave like short-legged gamebirds. Occasionally encountered alone, these sandgrouse are usually found in flocks that may exceed 100 birds. Their diet of grass seeds is especially dry, so flocks routinely seek water twice a day – at first light and again late in the afternoon – preferring shallow, open puddles. In the air they are vulnerable to predation by fast-flying birds of prey, especially the Lanner Falcon. Male birds look very smart with their yellow throats bordered with a black chinstrap, while females are suitably camouflaged for incubation duties. Listen out for the charming call of these sandgrouse, a gargled "*a-coo-coowoowoo*".

Lilac-breasted Roller

Eurasian Roller

Rollers get their name from the exuberant 'rolling' display flights in which they perform an impressive 'loop-the-loop'.

Male

In the breeding season, males soak their absorbent belly feathers in water and return to the nest where the chicks can then draw the moisture.

Female

Lilac-breasted Roller 38 cm 15″

A spectacular perching bird with a kaleidoscope of colours. Among the most popular of all birds in the Mara, this crow-sized jewel can be found across the reserve and is often located on a prominent tree branch over grassland from which it drops onto its favoured prey of beetles, grasshoppers and other invertebrates. In flight, it reveals brilliant blue feathers in the wings. These rollers nest in tree holes and are very territorial, chasing mammals and other birds, including huge eagles, away from the nest area. This is when you are most likely to hear their throaty "*kerr-kerr-kerr*" call. Adults are easily identified from the migrant Eurasian Roller by the long streamers at the sides of the tail, although these are lacking in the duller immature birds.

▶

Eurasian Roller
31 cm 12¼″

A colourful seasonal migrant to the Mara. At first glance this roller appears similar to the resident Lilac-breasted Roller but can quickly be separated by its all-blue head, throat and breast and, in flight, a richer chestnut 'saddle' on the back. The tail is also shorter and lacks the long tail streamers. The Eurasian Roller arrives from Europe during the October– November rains, when the plumage can appear 'washed out' or pale. After heading to southern Africa for several months it returns north again in March and April, when its colours are bright and fresh. Although vocal on their breeding grounds, they are generally silent in the Mara.

▼

Red-billed Oxpecker 22 cm 8½"

A red-billed 'tick-bird' found on mammals. Both species of oxpecker can be found on a variety of mammal species from which they famously collect ticks and other skin parasites. However, this apparently symbiotic relationship is not always what it seems. For as well as feasting on a variety of skin parasites and, strangely, ear-wax, oxpeckers are very happy to open wounds and drink the blood of the host, especially Hippos, which are frequently scarred and wounded in territorial fights. Although bill colour is the obvious feature used to separate the species, Red-billed Oxpeckers also have a yellow eye-ring and a uniform brown back, rump and tail (Yellow-billed Oxpeckers have an obviously pale rump).

Yellow-billed Oxpecker

20 cm 8"

A yellow-and-red-billed 'tick-bird' found on mammals. The bill colour and pale rump, which contrasts noticeably with the darker tail and back, separate this species from the similar Red-billed Oxpecker. Both species nest in tree holes, which are occasionally stolen from other birds. Immatures of the two species could be confused, as both have dark bills, but Yellow-billed Oxpeckers always show a pale rump. The sexes look similar in both species.

▼

Wattled Starling 20 cm 8″

This rather drab grey starling is a seasonal migrant, large flocks arriving from their breeding grounds in the Rift Valley with the annual Wildebeest migration. Although often seen riding the backs of various mammals, they prefer to feed on the invertebrates disturbed by the game rather than directly off the game itself (unlike the oxpeckers). In flight, they are easily identified by their white rumps that contrast with their black flight and tail feathers. A close up-view will reveal a bright-yellow skin patch behind the eye – but the saggy black wattles of the breeding males, from which this bird gets its name, are rarely seen in the Mara, where they are non-breeding visitors only.

Non-breeding

Breeding

Elephants are the only large mammals that will not tolerate oxpeckers on their skin, since it is very sensitive to the sharp claws of these birds.

Rufous-naped Lark 18 cm 7"

The common, chunky, brown-streaked lark of long grass plains. This drab-looking bird is frequently encountered on drives through the grassy plains when it springs up from tracks and verges, displaying an obvious chestnut wing patch – the only lark in the Mara to show this. Sometimes, birds will run in front of vehicles and avoid taking flight. If so, look out for the obvious crest. The song of this bird is the quintessential sound of the grassy plains, a pleasant whistled "*see-seeuu*" which translates usefully to "hey Joey". The similar Crested and Red-winged Larks do not occur in the reserve.

Rather bizarrely and despite the bird's name, it is very rare to see a rufous nape, the feathers behind the neck, on this species.

Pectoral-patch Cisticola ▶
9 cm 3½"

A tiny darting bird of long grass plains. At only 9 cm from bill to tail, this is the smallest of the grassland birds – but what it lacks in size it makes up for in energy and abundance. Many pairs occupy a square kilometre of grassland and males are often seen displaying by flying at breakneck speed over the grass and shooting up in the air while making sharp "*chit chit*" clicking sounds before dropping down into cover.

Red-capped Lark
15 cm 6"

An attractive small lark with a preference for short grass plains. The rich-rufous cap and chest patches on this bird contrast with the otherwise plain plumage, making it easily separable from the streak-breasted Rufous-naped Lark. Young birds are greyish and heavily peppered with pale feather edges. In flight, the tail appears very dark but shows lighter brown outer tail feathers. The simple call comprises a series of dry "*chirrp*" notes. It is often found with the Buffy Pipit (*page 58*).

Given a good view, look for the dark patches at the side of the chest, brown crown, and long legs if seen on open ground.

◼ **Buffy Pipit** 17 cm 6½″ ▶

The common nondescript pipit of open grassland. A very erect, long-legged bird that habitually makes short dashes before braking suddenly with a pumped tail. The back is quite plain and the breast and belly are whitish, although some birds show a warm buffy patch along the flanks. The flight is strong and reveals off-white outer tail feathers. The similar Grassland Pipit, which also occurs in the Mara, is more heavily striped on the back and breast and shows clean white outer tail feathers in flight.

Pipits can be a difficult group of birds to identify and until recently, the Buffy Pipits of the Mara were considered to be a subspecies of Plain-backed Pipit – so be aware that few field guides show Buffy Pipit occurring in this part of Kenya.

Immature male – same individual as below

◼ **Rosy-breasted Longclaw** ▶
20 cm 8″

A beautiful pink-fronted bird of long grass plains. Less common and far shyer than the Yellow-throated Longclaw, the male Rosy-breasted is one the prettiest birds in the Mara. Females and immatures show less pink than adult males but all birds have whiter edges to the back and flight feathers than the Yellow-throated, giving the bird a more scalloped appearance. A white bar in the wing can often be seen in flight.

Immature male

◻ Yellow-throated Longclaw 22 cm 8¾"

A yellow-breasted, terrestrial bird with a preference for long grass plains. It is common across the Mara and easily identified by its bright plumage. Females and immatures are duller than males but still show some yellow on the front. Birds are often seen along tracks and are easily flushed into the air when they glide on sharply flicked, flat wings and reveal two white squares on the end of the tail. They can be difficult to follow in the grass when they have their brown, streaked backs facing you. The high-pitched call "*wi-pi-pi-pi*" is frequently heard in flight.

Longclaws get their name from the very long claw at the back of the foot

Male

Female

■ Capped Wheatear   17 cm 6¾″

An attractive chat of short grass plains. With its distinctive face pattern and upright stance, the Capped Wheatear is difficult to confuse with any of the other resident birds. It is found singly or in pairs in areas of open, short grass with scattered rocks, often close to Maasai villages. It routinely bobs and pumps its tail. In flight, birds show an obvious white rump that contrasts with an all-black tail; this distinctive pattern is noticeable from afar. The sexes look similar. Two other wheatears, Northern and Isabelline, are common seasonal migrants from Europe but neither shows an all-black tail and both lack the clear face pattern of the Capped Wheatear.

▼

■ Northern Anteater Chat
18 cm 7″

All-dark perching birds with a white flash in the flight feathers. In the Mara, Northern Anteater Chats are less common than the similar Sooty Chat, and are usually encountered in extended family groups, rather than in pairs around termite mounds. Good areas to find them are close to Keekorok Lodge in the south of the reserve, and Serena Lodge in the Mara Triangle. Unlike the Sooty Chat, the sexes of this species are similar and easily identified by the extensive white patches in the flight feathers and otherwise chocolate-brown plumage.

▼

Territorial males will hold their wings down and raise their tail when singing.

Northern Anteater Chat

Sooty Chat

■ Sooty Chat 18 cm 7″

Small, dark birds of open areas. When perched, the glossy black males show an obvious white patch on the 'shoulders', though this is lacking in the browner females. Very similar in both appearance and behaviour to the Northern Anteater Chat. The two species are best separated in flight: male Sooty Chats show a bold white patch at the front of the wing and the females have no white in the wing at all; Northern Anteater Chats of both sexes show lots of white in the flight feathers (towards the end of the open wing). Pairs of Sooty Chat are usually found around large termite mounds, where they nest in the burrows of subterranean mammals. In Kenya, this bird is only found in the Mara.

Female

Male

Yellow Bishop 15 cm 6″

Short-tailed, black birds with bright-yellow flashes of the grassland edge. Males are very similar to Yellow-mantled Widowbird and both have black body plumage with a yellow 'shoulder' patch. However, male Yellow Bishops always show a bright yellow rump in all plumages and never a long, black tail. Yellow Bishops are more likely to be encountered close to water and in areas of tall, wet grass. Here you are likely to see their energetic display flight, which involves jumping from a perch and flapping rapidly before dropping down. During this show, males puff up their yellow rumps and call a rapid high-pitched *"tli-tli-tli-tli"*.

▼

Bishops are named after the red robes of bishops, the plumage of the males of many species in this group being red-and-black. The Yellow Bishop is one of several exceptions, being mostly black with yellow, rather than red.

Jackson's Widowbird ▶
30 cm 12″

Dark birds of long grass plains with long, drooping tails. The Mara is home to a very important population of these scarce birds that depend on large tracts of moist, open grassland. Breeding males are blackish with brown 'shoulder' patches and a sickle-shaped tail. Look out for displaying birds between February and June (during the second rains) when they fly up from the long grass before parachuting down again. Females and non-breeding males are brown and stripy and incredibly difficult to separate from other female and non-breeding male widowbirds and bishops. Flocks are often seen flying, squadron-like, several feet above the grass. This species is endemic to East Africa (*i.e.* it is only found here).

Male

Female

Yellow Bishop
Non-breeding
male

Display flight

Widowbirds are named after their black 'lady-in-mourning' plumage.

◻ Yellow-mantled Widowbird 21 cm 8¼"

Long-tailed, black birds of the long grass plains, with bright-yellow flashes. Pairs and small groups are often flushed from long grass quite unexpectedly and will often perch on small bushes. In flight, the yellow upper back and 'shoulder' patches of the breeding male help to separate it from Jackson's Widowbird (*above*) and other wandering widowbirds such as White-winged Widowbird (which shows a yellow 'shoulder' and a white upperwing patch) and Fan-tailed Widowbird (which has a red 'shoulder' and upperwing patch). As with Jackson's Widowbird, females and non-breeding males can be very difficult to identify with certainty.

Named after Sir Frederick Jackson (1859–1929), an English administrator, explorer and ornithologist who became the first Governor of Kenya.

Jackson's Widowbird
Female

☐ African Open-billed Stork 81 cm 32″

An all-dark stork with a large bill. These are non-breeding seasonal wanderers that arrive in vast flocks, sometimes numbering thousands, when the marshes are wet. They are specialist snail-feeders that use their stout bills, which show an obvious gap near the tip, to crack open the shells like a set of nutcrackers before manoeuvring the soft mollusc down the throat. In flight, flocks soar on flat wings, when they bear an uncanny resemblance to a prehistoric pterodactyl. The closest breeding colonies are on Lake Victoria but our visiting birds are more likely to arrive from larger colonies across central Africa.

▼

Although the bill shape is unique among African storks, there is also an Asian Open-billed Stork found across India and south-east Asia.

☐ Woolly-necked Stork
86 cm 34″

An unobtrusive dark stork with a white neck and belly. This bird is relatively scarce in the Mara, with just a few resident pairs that are joined by wandering birds between June and November. The lower reaches of the Mara River, especially below Lookout Hill, and along small rivers in the eastern conservancies are a good place to look. When seen standing, look out for the purple gloss on the back of this bird. In flight, the white neck separates it from the similar Abdim's Stork (*page 35*), which is a similar size and also has a white rump.

◄

Woolly-necked Stork

Yellow-billed Stork

☐ **Yellow-billed Stork** 108 cm 42″

A distinctive pied stork with a red face and long, yellow bill. This is a common resident of open marsh and rivers, where it is usually found resting in a hunched position or wading in shallow water in search of prey. It hunts a variety of aquatic creatures, including fish and amphibians, by moving its bill slowly in the water until it feels a food item. The bill is then snapped shut and the prey swallowed. This bird is not beyond piracy, so take time to enjoy these storks when in the company of small herons and egrets who are often cajoled into giving up their well-earned fish! In flight, they appear mostly white but reveal black flight and tail feathers and long pink legs that extend well beyond the tail. Like most storks, the sexes look similar, though immature birds are greyer all-over and lack the adults' brightly coloured bill.

Look out for the distinctive wing pattern in flying adult birds which look very graceful.

■ Saddle-billed Stork
145 cm 57"

A large, pied stork of marshy areas with a huge, red-and-black bill. The name comes from the bright-yellow leathery saddle on top of the bill, rather than the upturned shape of the bill itself. Although these storks are not present in large numbers in the Mara, they are easy to identify on account of their distinctive plumage, and are a favourite with guides and visitors alike. Solitary birds can be often be found wading through wet grass searching for frogs and catfish, and it can be great fun watching them tackle larger prey. Males have a dark eye and females a yellow eye, and both have bright-pink 'knee-caps' which gives the impression that someone has attached a sticking plaster to each leg! Young birds are greyish and their bill is shorter and lacks the colour of an adult. At this age, the bird bears a passing resemblance to the amazing Shoebill, (*not shown*) a rare stork from the papyrus swamps of Uganda and Tanzania, which has occurred only once in the Mara. It can take two years to reach maturity, during which time they gradually attain their clean black-and-white plumage and yellow saddle.

■ Sacred Ibis 73 cm 29"

A wandering bird of the wetlands that can sometimes be seen in flocks of 20 or more. The general impression of an ibis is that it has a rather 'horizontal' posture, especially in comparison to the 'vertical' storks and herons that they superficially resemble. They are generally active feeders and will walk around wet and grassy areas probing their thick, strongly decurved bill in search of frogs, fish and invertebrates. The head of adult birds is jet-black and lacks feathers, but immature birds can show some white mottling on the face and neck. In flight, birds often show bare, red skin along the front of the underwings, making them appear quite prehistoric.

The bird acquired its Sacred name on account of its religious status among the Pharaohs of ancient Egypt who worshipped the bird in the form of the God they named Thoth. In Saqqara, in one excavated tomb alone, 1,500,000 mummified ibises were discovered!

■ Hadada Ibis 82 cm 32"

A noisy brown ibis of river, marsh and, sometimes, open woodland. The bird gets its name from the very loud calls that are usually the first clue to its presence – a raucous "*haa-ha-haa*," or sometimes a single drawn out "*haaaaa*". On first impression, the bird can appear a bland brown, but sit and watch and the sunlight reflecting off the wings may reveal a stunning glossy sheen of blue, green, purple and copper; this can often be seen clearly when the bird is in flight. Like the Sacred Ibis, Hadada will spend much of their time walking and probing for food. Adult birds show a whitish eye and a pale moustache extending from the red-topped bill. Look out for the similar, but scarce, Glossy Ibis which is a much slimmer, darker brown version with longer legs and an all-dark bill.

These birds are very much at home in the company of people, and across southern Africa are commonly found in gardens and parks.

◀ ☐ Squacco Heron 46 cm 18″

A small, pale heron of open marshes with white wings. Although not common in the Mara, the Squacco Heron is most likely to be found on the edges of open water, especially at Musiara Marsh in the north of the reserve, and is easy to identify given a good view. Appearing short and bull-necked, birds in breeding plumage are beige with long, cinnamon plumes down the back and a series of black and white plumes emerging from the neck. Immature and non-breeding birds are typically more streaky and have a darker brown back. In flight, birds of all ages show snow-white wings and tail that contrast with the browner colouration of the back. The nearest breeding colonies are at Lake Baringo in the northern Rift Valley.

☐ Striated Heron 40 cm 15¾″

A small, dark heron of pools and quiet rivers. Its body plumage is mostly grey but it shows pale feather edges, subtle white stripes in the face and a black cap that is erected when the bird is excited or agitated. In the breeding season, its legs change from yellow to pink. Immature birds are similar but heavily streaked on the throat ▶ and spotted on the back and wings. In flight, the short legs and tail are obvious, and this is when you are most likely to hear its call – a short, sharp, barking growl. Although widespread across much of Kenya, the Mara is one of only a few regular nesting sites for this species.

◀ ☐ Rufous-bellied Heron

46 cm 18″

A scarce small, dark heron of quiet marshes. The Rufous-bellied Heron is a rare bird in Kenya and only reliably encountered in the Mara, where it is a resident of the ox-bow lakes and permanent swamps close to Governors' Camp and Kichwa Tembo. It is a dark, sooty-brown heron that reveals rich chestnut plumage on the belly and underwing in flight, when the bright-yellow legs are most obvious. The bill is also yellow with a dark tip, which helps to separate it from the Striated Heron. Young birds appear scruffy and also paler on the throat. This is a great bird to find by any birdwatcher's standards!

Usually encountered in a hunched position, the Striated, or Green-backed Heron, is a shy bird that prefers keeping to cover around water.

☐ Great White Egret
92 cm 36"

A large, elegant and long-necked white heron of quiet waterways. Unlike the Cattle Egret, this is a solitary bird rarely seen away from water Although the largest of the white egrets, attention still needs to be paid in order to secure a positive identification. Look out for the long neck that should show a strong kink, sometimes two, and the line of the bill opening, known as the gape, which extends below and well behind the eye. As with other egrets, the plumage varies slightly according to the time of year. Birds in breeding plumage show a greenish patch of skin at the base of a black bill, long white plumes flowing from the back and breast, and yellowish legs. Non-breeding birds have an all-yellow bill, blacker legs and lack the elegant white plumes.

Little Egret

Great White Egret

Egrets derive their name from the French word *aigrette*, meaning brush, on account of the long filamentous plumes they acquire in the breeding season.

Look out for flocks of Cattle Egrets gathering at the feet of Buffalo where they feed on the invertebrates disturbed by the mammals, whose backs they frequently ride.

Breeding

◀ ▣ Cattle Egret 56 cm 22″

A small, short-necked, white egret that associates with grazing animals. Often found on the grassy plains where they feed among herds of Buffalo, Elephant and other large grazers, these egrets will routinely visit rivers and marshes, where they preen and roost. It is here where they may be confused with other egrets that are associated with water, but this is the only egret that habitually gathers in large flocks. Cattle Egrets have far shorter necks than the other species shown here, and are usually seen hunched when roosting. In breeding plumage, birds develop bright-orange tones to the crest and chest, and the facial skin turns bright-red. At this time, the legs are orange, while non-breeding birds show black legs and all-white plumage.

Cattle Egret
Non-breeding

◀ ▣ Little Egret
64 cm 25″

A medium-sized, white heron with a slim, black bill. The Little Egret is a delicate bird of open marshes, rivers and ponds that has many similarities with the Great White Egret. However, it always shows black legs with bright-yellow feet, and a fine, black bill that contrasts with a yellow patch of skin in front of the eyes. A good view will also reveal a long, elegant crest. This species has a rarely seen 'dark morph' plumage that is slaty-grey all-over except for a white chin.

71

☐ Goliath Heron 152 cm 60″

A huge, chestnut-headed and grey-backed heron of quiet waters. With its huge, dagger-shaped bill and gigantic proportions, this really is an impressive bird by anyone's standards. In flight, look out for the rich-chestnut underwing and very broad wings. It is not likely to be confused with any other bird and all good safari guides will know it well. Take time to enjoy this bird fishing and, if it appears to be resting, you may be lucky enough to watch it sunbathing, when it stands facing the sun with its wings held half-open.

▶

The Goliath Heron is the largest heron in the world and named after the biblical giant defeated by David.

☐ Black-headed Heron 92 cm 36"

A mostly dark, medium-sized heron of marshes and plains. Smaller and darker than the Grey Heron, this species shows a white throat that contrasts markedly with the darker head and back of the neck. In flight, the upperwing is darker than in Grey Heron and the underwing shows an obvious contrast between the white coverts (front half of wing) and blackish flight feathers (back half of wing). Often found on open marshes with other herons, the Black-headed is also readily seen walking the grassy plains in search of lizards and snakes. Because this heron has a slower and less deadly approach to killing snakes, than the Secretarybird, for example, it is not uncommon to see the snake wrapping itself around the bird's bill ▶ – making for spectacular wildlife viewing.

Grey Heron

Black-headed Heron

◀ ☐ Grey Heron 100 cm 38"

A large, white-and-grey heron of open water and marsh. Adult birds are easily identified by their whitish head, neck and belly, and sport long, black feathers that extend from above the eye down the back of the neck. Immature birds show more grey in the face and lack the adults' black facial plumes. In flight, birds show darker flight feathers on the upperwing, while the underwing is uniform grey with no contrast. An accomplished fisherman, the Grey Heron is not beyond taking other prey such as reptiles, young birds and small mammals. The commonly heard call is a loud "*fronk*".

☐ African Fish Eagle 73 cm 29″

A stunning large eagle of river and marsh. The quintessential sound of African waterways, the loud cry of the African Fish Eagle is never to be forgotten – adult birds throw their necks back in joy as the yelping "*weeoww-ow-ow*" call pierces the sky. The distinctive plumage of adult birds should pose no issues with identification. However, immature birds can appear a strange mix of brown and white patches, and only acquire the classic white head after several years. It is common to see these majestic birds soaring on broad wings over wet areas or perched on a conspicuous branch with water in view.

Although the main prey item is fish, these eagles will also take lizards and birds as large as flamingos.

Adult

Immature

A Hamerkop's call, usually given in flight, is a high-pitched "*chink-chink-chink*". This sounds like a hammer striking an anvil and this is how the bird acquired its local name of 'fundi chuma', the blacksmith.

☐ **Hamerkop** 56 cm 22″

A small brown hammer-headed heron. The Hamerkop (Dutch and Afrikaans for Hammer Head) is an oddity among African herons because of its all-brown colouration, peculiar head-shape and short legs. However, like other members of the heron family, it is an accomplished fisherman and is often found at the water's edge waiting for frogs and fish to come within striking distance. It also employs other tactics such as wiggling its feet in mud to stir up food items, and may even fly into the wind at low level and dip at the water's surface to pick off unsuspecting fish. This bird builds a huge nest in a strong tree to which it adds new extensions year after year. These constructions offer apartments for other birds, such as sparrows and weavers, and once neglected by the owners, are frequently taken over by Grey Kestrels and other species.

Thick-knees are also known as dikkops across much of southern Africa, while the migratory Eurasian Thick-knee, a very rare visitor to the Mara, is also known as the Stone-curlew.

They are very spirited birds and show great valour when defending their eggs and chicks against predators, such as huge monitor lizards, by opening their wings and making darting runs to intimidate them.

Water Thick-knee
41 cm 16"

A small, shy wading bird of the water's edge. Although quite common in the Mara, these birds can be tricky to find as they prefer to sit motionless rather than fly away from danger or disturbance. If seen well on the ground, look out for the crouched, horizontal posture, large yellow eyes and green legs. Once airborne, the open wings show large white patches. Birds become very active after dark and this is when they are most likely to be heard, screaming a long series of excited "*wee*" notes, starting quickly and rising to a crescendo; this sometimes involves several individuals.

☐ Spur-winged Goose   100 cm 39"

An unmistakable large, pied goose with a white face and pink legs. This is a regular visitor to the flooded grasslands of the Mara, especially at Musiara and in the Mara Triangle. The black on the back and neck appears glossy green in strong light, contrasting heavily with the white belly. At close range, look out for the warty face of the male and a fleshy red knob on the forehead. In flight, the black upperwing has a white leading-edge and the underwing shows black flight feathers against white. Often calls in flight, a hiccup-like "*ku-wup-up*".

▶

Egyptian Goose

Spur-winged Goose

The Spur-winged Goose is not popular among hunters on account of its bad-tasting flesh.

☐ Egyptian Goose ▶

74 cm 29"

A common, light-brown goose with a dark eye-patch. It is a regular feature on game drives that include rivers and marsh. This attractive goose probably looks its best in flight, when it show a large white panel on the upperwing and iridescent green inner flight feathers. Despite their rather serene appearance, these geese can be very aggressive and fights are common where territorial incursions occur. Intruders are threatened with open wings in a show of intimidation followed by noisy honking that quickens in excitement.

White-faced Whistling Duck 48 cm 19"

A gregarious brown waterfowl with a white face.
Usually encountered in small flocks, this
medium-sized, upright duck is at home along
the grassy margins of open marsh and quiet
rivers, but less so along the busy stretches
of the Mara River. These ducks have a very
distinctive call, a sweetly whistled "*wer-wi-wooo*",
which you are likely to hear before you see them.
They are long-necked and long-legged, and a good
view will present no identification problems. However,
distant birds in flight could be confused with the Fulvous ▶
Whistling Duck (*not shown*), though that species lacks
the white face and is a paler chestnut-brown on the head,
breast and belly. If you see a white crescent on the rump
in flight then it is definitely a Fulvous. The sexes look
similar in both species.

Whistling Ducks are sometimes called Tree
Ducks in the Americas. However, their
scientific name *Dendrocygna* means 'tree
swan' – all rather confusing considering
that they are actually more closely related
to geese than either ducks or swans!

The frequently seen
goslings are soft and
downy, patched with
brown-and-white,
but soon turn scruffy
brown with age.

▪ African Jacana 31 cm 12¼"

An attractive waterbird with incredibly long toes. Commonly known as the Lily-trotter on account of its habit of walking on floating vegetation, especially water-lilies, the African Jacana shows an attractive blue bill and shield on the forehead. Its breeding behaviour is particularly strange because the typical roles of the sexes are reversed. The larger females are outrageously flirtatious and frequently mate with several partners. The smaller males are the ones who build the nest, incubate the eggs and rear the young, quite independently of the female. This rare behaviour is known as polyandry. Look out for them in weak fluttering flight when they appear to be 'all-feet'.

▶

▪ Black-winged Stilt 38 cm 15" ▶

A very long-legged, elegant, pied wader of open marshes. Needless to say, their extra-long, rosy-pink legs explain the name 'stilt' and enable them to feed in deeper water than other wading birds of the same size. Although not resident in the Mara, it is not unusual to see them wading gracefully through shallow water, dipping their long, thin bill from side to side or picking insects off grass stems. In flight, they are not easy to confuse, the simple plumage of all-white head and body contrasting sharply with the black wings – and those gangly legs extending well beyond the tail. Immatures are similar but are browner and have duller legs. The distinctive call is a dripping "*kip-kip-kip*".

Some adult birds show a dark smudge on the head

Black Crake
20 cm 8″

A shy black bird of the water's edge. These small birds rarely allow prolonged views or a close approach but, if seen well, look out for the bright yellow bill and pink legs. They prefer to remain hidden in dense vegetation but lucky observers may see them on the backs of Hippo where they feed on skin parasites. When trying to locate this bird, listen out for the unmistakable call, a muffled, dove-like "*crr-crrr-crrr-coo*".

☐ Long-toed Plover

31 cm 12¼"
A scarce pied plover with an all-grey back and red legs. This bird is restricted to open, wet marshes where it feeds along the water's edge and on floating vegetation. Although superficially similar to the other pied plovers, this is the only species to show a white forehead, face and throat, together with a red-and-black bill and red legs. It appears taller than the other pied plovers on account of its longer legs and neck. In flight, this is the only plover to show a completely white forewing on the upperside. Its ratchety call sounds similar to an African moped, or 'piki piki', that's having trouble starting! Regularly seen at Musiara, near Governors' Camp.

▶

☐ Spur-winged Plover 28 cm 11" ▶

A common pied plover with white cheeks and brown back. This plover is simple to identify because of its bold plumage – so you don't need to waste time searching for the bony spurs on the wings, after which it is named, as these are usually hidden. Even in flight, the white cheeks stand out against the dark breast but, if seen from above, look for the white bar running from the front to the back of the upperwing (*see page 32*).

In the Mara, it is regular along rocky river beds (try the 'Smelling River' crossing – your guide will know it), as well as a variety of marshes and along the Mara River. Its call is similar to, but higher pitched than, the Blacksmith Plover and often gets carried away with excitement, especially when mating.

Large plovers within the scientific genus *Vanellus*, including those on these pages and on *pages 33 & 85* are also known as lapwings

Blacksmith Plover 31 cm 12¼″
A common pied plover with a white forehead and black back. Less restricted to freshwater marshes than the Long-toed Plover, this bird may also be found on the edge of the plains and along the rivers of the Mara reserve. It is the only plover to show black cheeks extending to the breast. In flight, it appears mostly grey-and-black and also shows a white rump contrasting with the black tail – the latter is a feature common to most species in this genus. The name derives from its call which, like the Hamerkop, sounds like a hammer striking an anvil: "*tink-tink-tink*". It is thought to be declining in some areas due to competition from Spur-winged Plover, which is expanding its range.

This is the largest of the migratory sandpipers that visit the Mara from northern Europe and is usually found here from September until April but some birds stay all year.

Three-banded Plover
18 cm 7″

A small plover with two – not three – dark bands across the breast. If you are wondering why it is called Three-banded Plover, just remember that the white band between the two black ones also counts! This attractive little wader, with its bright red eye-rings and pink legs, is often very confiding and accepting of a close approach, especially in muddy roadside pools. It is also common along sandy river banks where your attention may be drawn to its very high-pitched "*phew-eet*" contact call. When very excited it calls a long muffled "*wi-wi-sher-wir-wirrit*" that sounds swift-like.

Common Greenshank 32 cm 12½"

A medium-sized, elegant wader of the water's edge. This mostly grey-brown sandpiper is very pale on the underparts and always shows green legs, or shanks – hence the name. The long bill, showing an obvious upward curve, gets darker towards the tip and is used in a swinging fashion through the water. Greenshanks are energetic feeders and will often run through the shallows chasing small fish and invertebrates. In flight they appear dark above and pale below with an obvious white triangle running up the back. The resonant "*chew-chew-chew*" call is very distinctive and often alerts you to the bird well before you've seen it.

African Wattled Plover
34 cm 13½"

A large, brown plover with distinctive facial skin. In some respects similar to the pied plovers on the previous page, the African Wattled Plover lacks the heavy patches of black and white, and appears uniform brown from a distance. Close inspection reveals a delicately streaked head and neck, and spectacular yellow wattles hanging from between the eyes and the bill. This is complemented by a yellow bill tipped with black, and long, yellow legs. The wattles of male birds are generally longer than those of females but otherwise the sexes look similar. This plover is less restricted to open water than similar species and is often at home close to puddles and wet grass. Calling birds usually start with a prolonged series of high-pitched "*wherp*" notes but when several individuals join in excitedly it can quicken to "*wit-wit-wit-wu*".

If you're not 100% certain about your identification, check the brown plovers found on the plains (*page 33*).

General note: these small sandpipers are all seasonal migrants from Europe and can be difficult to separate. Pay particular attention to their calls and the following three features when observing them: rump and tail pattern; leg colour; and the degree of contrast between the upperparts and underparts.

Green Sandpiper 23 cm 9″

A stocky sandpiper of quiet waters. The Green Sandpiper is most similar to Wood Sandpiper but shows far greater contrast between the dark back and wings, which have little in the way of flecking in them, and the white belly. The face is usually quite dark, making the white eye-ring very clear if seen well; it lacks the pale eyebrow extending beyond the eye, which is a feature of Wood Sandpiper. Both the bill and the legs are dark and greenish. In flight, birds appear blackish, especially on the underwing, and show a contrasting clean white rump and three to four strong black bars running across the end of the tail. Rising birds call a piercing "*tlu-EET-wit-wit*" that is far more abrupt than the Wood Sandpiper.

Common Sandpiper 20 cm 8″

A small, short-legged, hunched sandpiper with a brown tail and rump. It is a migrant and occurs commonly between August and May, being found mainly along boulder-strewn streams, although birds will also visit wider rivers and marshes. It stands with a horizontal posture and walks with a bobbing action, regularly 'pumping' its rear-end. Unlike the other two sandpipers shown here, the Common Sandpiper's tail projects well beyond the wing-tips. The belly is crisp white with no barring on the flanks, and a white patch cuts up towards the shoulder. It has a low, pulsating flight action with the wings arched slightly downwards. It lacks a white rump and shows a uniform brown colour across the back and down the tail, which is often spread and appears pointed in the centre. The open wing shows a long, narrow white bar down the middle. The call is a very high-pitched long series of "*swee-swee-swee*" notes.

Wood Sandpiper 20 cm 8″

A refined sandpiper of flooded grass, rivers and marshes. Wood Sandpipers are far more numerous than Green Sandpipers and are often, but not always, encountered in extended groups. They lack the strong contrast in plumage of the Green Sandpiper primarily because the back and wings are heavily flecked with pale feather edgings and the sides of the belly also carry some soft barring. This combines to give the bird a more streaked appearance and less 'black-and-white'. The bright yellowish-green legs are a very useful identification feature. In flight, they show a pale-grey underwing and a gentle intergrade between the mottled back and the white rump, while the tail shows several narrow soft bars. The monotone call "*chif-if-if*" is a common feature of wet areas throughout much of the year but birds become scarce between May and August.

This is the largest of the world's 95 species of kingfisher.

Giant Kingfisher 43 cm 17″

A huge, chequered kingfisher of larger waterways. Generally scarce and shy, the Giant Kingfisher is about the size of a crow and has a thick, shaggy crest at the back of the head. Males show a chestnut-red breast-band, whereas females have a chestnut-coloured belly. It is quite at home along the Mara River, where it hunts fish, crabs and amphibians by diving from a perch. It is easily disturbed and calls a loud "*kark*" note often in flight.

Male

Female

◀ ■ **Malachite Kingfisher** 12 cm 4¾″
A brilliant blue-and-red jewel of still and
slow-moving water. Despite its tiny size,
the Malachite Kingfisher causes gasps
of amazement because of its stunning
plumage. Sometimes found balancing
from a grass stem hanging over a small
pool, it sits and watches for any small
fish or tasty morsel to surface, snatching
it with a rapid dive. It then proceeds to
slam the unfortunate fish on its perch to
kill it and make swallowing it, head first,
easier. Otherwise, a flash of brilliant colour
whizzing along the water at top speed is
the typical view. The nest is made at the
end of a long tunnel in a sandbank. The
simple call is a soft high-pitched "*peep*".

▲
■ **Pied Kingfisher** 25 cm 10″
A common black-and-white
kingfisher of open water. Regularly
seen hovering over rivers and
marshes, the Pied Kingfisher is quite
unmistakable and not at all shy.
Pairs and family parties are often
seen together and their metallic
"*chit*" contact calls are frequently
heard in unison. Males are
easily told from females by their
two solid black bands across the
chest; females show just a single,
broken band. It is among the most
cosmopolitan of all kingfishers,
being found in south-eastern
Europe and across southern Asia to
China, as well as throughout Africa.

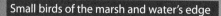

◄ ☐ Moustached Grass Warbler
19 cm 7½"

A large, brown warbler of rank vegetation, usually close to moving water. Unlike many brown warblers, this one has pale eyes and such distinctive face markings that it is easy to identify. You are quite likely to encounter it in camps and lodges where the habitat is suitable, especially at Kichwa Tembo. It is quite boisterous and sings loudly from an open perch – a loud burst that has been translated usefully to "*chirp-chirp-chirp, doesn't it tickle you?*" With so many LBJs – little brown jobs – in the Mara that defy identification and prompt many a yawn, beginners are encouraged to start by enjoying the easy ones first, including this little beauty. It was formerly called African Moustached Warbler.

☐ African Pied Wagtail ►
20 cm 8"

A small, black-and-white bird with a long tail, commonly found along the edge of rivers. These dainty birds with striking plumage habitually pump their tails when perched and when walking. The frequently heard call is a strong, whistled "*chereep-chup-chup-chup*", sometimes ending "*watcha watcha*".

Other wagtails of the Mara include the rarely seen Mountain Wagtail, (*not shown*) which is found along forested streams, and the migratory Yellow Wagtail (*not shown*), whose many forms often accompany grazing animals on short, wet grassland between September and March.

Common Waxbill 10cm 4"

A masked 'finch' of both wet and dry grassland, often close to water. Usually encountered in flocks dangling from grassy seed-heads, these dainty little birds show a bright-red waxy-looking bill, red bandit's mask and white on the chin. Otherwise they are mostly brown, though a close-up view will reveal fine barring throughout and a black belly. They are widespread in the Mara but move seasonally in search of the best seeding grasses – so if you see one you're likely to see many.

Waxbills are very popular cage birds and many have escaped from captivity in various parts of the world. They now live wild in Brazil, Spain and Portugal and on many small islands in the Atlantic, Pacific and Indian Oceans.

Unlike many other eagles, snake eagles have mostly bare legs that are useful when tackling dangerous snakes.

◀ ☐ Brown Snake Eagle 71 cm 28″

A medium-sized, brown eagle with an owl-like face. The dark chocolate-brown plumage appears uniform when the bird is perched, scanning for reptiles and snakes. It has a rounded head and forward-facing bright-yellow eyes. In flight it looks plain from above but shows very pale, almost silvery, flight feathers from below. Immature birds tend to be paler on the face but are otherwise similar to adults.

◀ ☐ Long-crested Eagle 58 cm 23″

The only dark-brown raptor with a long crest. Although this small, compact eagle has a preference for open woodland, it can also be encountered on the plains, when its distinctive silhouette may be seen as it perches on top of a tree. It watches patiently before dropping down to prey upon reptiles and small mammals. In addition to the long, floppy crest, its bare parts are bright-yellow and it sports short, white 'trousers'. It has a peculiar flapping flight on straight wings, which show a large white patch on the top and lots of white on the underside. The tail is dark with grey bars.

Even in a light wind, look for the floppy crest that looks like a crazy punk hairdo!

Long-crested Eagle

Brown Snake Eagle

African Hawk Eagle immature

African Hawk Eagle adult

As with most raptor species, the female is noticeably larger than the male.

☐ African Hawk Eagle ▶

66 cm 26″

A powerful, medium-sized, black-and-white eagle. This lethal raptor is a strong and stealthy hunter of gamebirds such as Helmeted Guineafowl and francolins, and mammals such as Scrub Hares. They frequently hunt in pairs and even in family parties once young birds have left the nest. Although uncommon in the Mara, they are seen regularly near the Ol Kiombo airstrip area where a pair usually breeds. In flight, it can be separated from other eagles by its mostly pale underwing that shows a distinct dark stripe running down the middle; immature birds show a light, rusty wash to the underparts and underwing.

93

◄ ☐ **Scaly Francolin** 31 cm 12¼"

A plain-looking francolin with a red bill and red legs. Like the Three-banded Plover (*page 84*), it would appear that this bird has been misnamed, as it does not look particularly scaly, especially when compared with the male Hildebrandt's Francolin, for example. It prefers to keep to cover but it is quite tame if stumbled upon when on foot. It is less vocal than the Red-necked Spurfowl and you're more likely to hear its soft purring "*kwoorr*" contact call than the louder "*ker-RAK-kerRAK*" territorial call. An average clutch is six eggs and these francolins have an unusual habit of incubating by night and deserting by day, perhaps to keep predators off the scent.

◄ ☐ **Red-necked Spurfowl**
38 cm 15"

A grey-brown francolin with red bare parts. Common in lightly wooded country towards the west of the reserve, this distinctive gamebird always shows a red bill and legs but only males exhibit the red skin on the neck. They are vocal birds, screaming out their territorial calls "*kwark-kwaark*" at any time of day. They do not have a defined breeding season and males can be seen chasing females at breakneck speed with open wings and great gusto – hilarious to watch! Not surprisingly, females lay several clutches of eggs each year.

Hildebrandt's Francolin
41 cm 16"

A large, shy francolin of dense cover. You will almost certainly hear this francolin before you see it – and heaven forbid that you are trying to nap when it gets going! The shrieking territorial call "*kik-kerik-kerik-kerik*" gets louder and louder and then, if you're really unlucky, the female joins in. These are the largest francolins in the Mara and appear more round than the others. Males are heavily spotted with black on the front and neck, while females are rich-brown on the belly.

▶

General note: The names spurfowl and francolin are often used interchangeably for the same species, the actual difference being minimal. In East Africa, the name spurfowl is given to those species that show bare throat skin, and francolin to those that do not. The South Africans take a different stance, with Scaly and Hildebrandt's Francolins being called Spurfowl. It's a funny old 'game'!

This bird was named in honour of Johann Maria Hildebrandt (1847–1881), a German collector who travelled extensively to East Africa, Madagascar and the Comoro Islands.

Male

Female

Coqui Francolin 28 cm 11″

A small, rusty-coloured francolin
of open scrub and grassland. This
beautifully marked gamebird is
often encountered on the edge of
plains where the bush thickens
into open woodland. Males are
rusty-brown on the head and
heavily barred underneath;
females show dark, painted
markings on the face and a rusty
breast. There is uncertainty about
how this francolin got its name,
but it probably stems from its
call, a repeated "*ko-kee*" that rises
to a crescendo. This is most often
heard in the late afternoon.
▼

Helmeted Guineafowl 61 cm 24″ ▶

A large, gregarious gamebird with finely
spotted plumage. Despite its bare blue-
and-red skinned face and bony helmet,
this is an attractive bird that feeds in the
open but needs trees nearby in which
to roost and take refuge from its many
predators. It is a favourite with small
cats, such as Serval, and stealthy birds
of prey such as the African Hawk Eagle.
The chicks exhibit rapid wing growth
and are able to fly from danger after just
one week out of the shell.

Female

Male

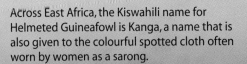

Across East Africa, the Kiswahili name for Helmeted Guineafowl is Kanga, a name that is also given to the colourful spotted cloth often worn by women as a sarong.

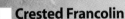

◀ ■ Crested Francolin
30 cm 12″

A stripy, bantam-like gamebird. This drab francolin has a preference for dry, open bush in the east of the reserve but does wander westwards from July. It often gathers in large family groups. The sexes look similar, although females sometimes appear more barred on the upperparts than males. The short crest, after which the bird is named, can be difficult to see unless birds are excited, but look out for the cocked tail that is usually raised.

Laughing Dove 23 cm 9″

A small, rufous-and-grey-winged dove. Common in drier areas, and often on open ground, this species still requires trees in which to nest and is rarely found far from cover. It lacks the black neck collar of the other doves shown here but has a black-and-rusty mottled patch high on the chest. In flight, it appears slender and shows large white corners to the long, dark-centred tail that are more obvious than those of Ring-necked Dove. It has a wide distribution, being found from south-western Europe, where it is also known as the Palm Dove, eastwards across much of Asia and most of Africa. Its call is a gentle giggling "*hoo-woo-woo-woo-woo*", hence the bird's name.

Red-eyed Dove 32 cm 12½″ ▶

A large, dark-brown dove with a black collar and a bright rosy flush. More restricted to woodland than the Ring-necked Dove, this species is a rich dark-brown on the back, has grey on the belly and, in flight, shows a smoky-grey tail with a thick blackish band across the middle. Although the red eye and eye-ring can be difficult to see, the pink flush to the neck and breast is obvious and contrasts with the white forehead. Its call is a bouncy series of purred notes that usefully translates to "*I am a Red-eyed Dove*", often repeated over and over.

◀ ▪ **Ring-necked Dove** 25 cm 10″
A common beige-coloured dove of lightly
wooded areas. The black collar at the back of
the neck, after which this bird is named, is
distinctive, but this feature is also shared with the
larger Red-eyed Dove and the African Mourning
Dove (*not shown*), the latter not being found in
the Mara. In flight, the upperwing shows a
pale-grey stripe which contrasts with the darker
flight feathers, and the light-brown tail has
white triangles at each corner which is a useful
aid when the bird flies away. The well-loved
call is one of the easiest of all to remember,
a softly purred "*pur-PUR-pur*", commonly
translated to "*work harder*" (mornings)
or "*more lager*" (evenings). It is
known as the Cape Turtle Dove
across southern Africa.

■ **Speckled Pigeon** 34 cm 13½"

A large, heavily spotted pigeon, common around villages surrounding the Mara, as well as in wooded gardens around camps and lodges. The brown wings are peppered with white spots and in flight the rump shows as pale-grey and the tail is bordered with black. The grey head shows a patch of bare red skin around the eyes and the chest is delicately streaked with maroon. Just like urban pigeons, this bird has a habit of clapping its wings on take-off.

▶

◄ ☐ **African Green Pigeon** 27 cm 10½"

A spectacular bright-green pigeon. Usually found feeding in the top of fruiting trees, especially fig, these gorgeous lime-green birds have a peculiar call that is quite unlike that of other pigeons and doves. It starts with a soft "*hoo-hoo-wee-oo*" followed by excited whinnying and a few yelped "*whip-hoo-woo-whip*" notes before ending softly with "*ku-KU-ku-ku*". If you're lucky enough to see it well, look out for the red bill with a white tip, red legs and lilac shoulder patch. As they depend on emerging fruits, birds will commute great distances from their roosting sites to visit favoured fruiting trees.

The infamously extinct Dodo of Mauritius in the Indian Ocean was a giant flightless pigeon, closely related to the green pigeons, which became island-bound as the commuting distance between island and mainland became too great over millions of years.

☐ **Emerald-spotted Wood Dove**
20 cm 8"

A small, colourful dove of dry, wooded areas, usually seen circling the woodland floor with an action similar to a clockwork toy. If disturbed, it shoots into the air with a rapid burst of wing-beats, showing chestnut flight feathers and a grey rump and tail with narrow black bars. The frequently heard call is a series of muffled "*coo*" notes that start with a rise (exactly like the first four notes of "*Rule Britannia*" for those that know it) before simultaneously falling in tone and speeding up, finishing on a rapid, pulsating flourish. This will make sense when you hear it! The glossy emerald wing-spots may appear black or shiny-blue in some lights, but be careful not to confuse this common bird with the Blue-spotted Wood Dove (*not shown*) that is found in wetter forests and has a dark-red bill with a yellow tip. ◄

■ Speckled Mousebird 33 cm 13″

A small-bodied brown bird with a long, stiff tail. This comical little bird is often seen clambering through bushes and thick vegetation, where it feeds on seeds and fruit. As its name suggests, it does appear quite mouse-like apart from in flight when its long tail is a useful identification feature. Good views will also reveal pale cheeks and pink feet. The call is a simple chatter, "*chir-chir-chir-chir-chir*" that drops in tone.

Formerly known as Coly-birds (the scientific genus remains *Colius*), these cute balls of feather were once given as gifts between the Lords, Ladies and gentry of the day. It is thought that the 'Four Calling Birds' alluded to in the *12 Days of Christmas* carol is a corruption from the original 'Four Coly-birds', but this changed over time because nobody knew what a Coly-bird was.

■ African Grey Hornbill

51 cm 20″

A medium-sized hornbill with a white eyebrow and scaly brown plumage. This bird prefers to feed in a variety of trees where it eats mostly fruits and invertebrates. It travels between trees and bushes with an undulating flight, when it looks like a flying walking stick on account of its slim lines and decurved bill. Birds stay in contact with long, piped calls "*kwi-kwi-kwi-KWEE-o-KWEE-o*". Their breeding behaviour is remarkable. Once a suitable nest hole in a tree is found, the female seals herself in to deter predators and nest-site rivals, using her droppings and other debris. She leaves a small slit through which the male feeds her during the period of incubation. When the young grow too large for comfort she leaves the nest and the chicks re-seal the entrance. Both adults then feed the chicks until they are ready to fledge.

Meyer's Parrot 23 cm 9" ▶

A small, brown parrot with a green belly and splashes of yellow, often seen in pairs and small family groups. Meyer's Parrot is also known as Brown Parrot, which seems a shame as it carries so many other bright colours. The noisy screeches in flight and when perched mean that you're unlikely to miss it if it's around. Young birds lack the yellow on the crown but are otherwise similar to adults. It is found where fruiting trees, especially the Kenya Greenheart, are located.

Named after Dr Bernhard Meyer (1767–1836) who was a physician by profession but a keen ornithologist in his spare time. Oddly, it is thought he never actually travelled to Africa where this species is found.

Many safari guides call this the water-bottle bird because of its distinctive call, a rapid series of bubbling "*woo-woo-woo-woo*" notes that fall before rising with a stammer at the end.

◀ ☐ White-browed Coucal 41 cm 16"

A bulky brown bird of wet and wooded areas. Closely related to the cuckoos, coucals raise their own young and make grassy, domed nests in tall grass or thick vegetation. They are weak fliers and rarely wander far from their territory. Coucals appear rather ungainly on the ground but spend much of their time walking stealthily through vegetation in search of a meal – this can include eggs and baby birds, and reptiles and amphibians. In addition to being good parents, they are also good at relationships and will pair for life. If one bird dies, the other will spend days mourning for its loved one.

◀ ☐ Bare-faced Go-away-bird
48 cm 19"

A large, pale-grey bird with a tall crest and long, broad tail. Often seen in pairs or groups, this go-away-bird does not scream "*Go Away*" like its southern African relative the Grey Go-away-bird. Instead it calls "*cor-cor*" very loudly and runs along the branches of trees in great excitement, often hopping from one to the next. The face is mostly black and the tall, grey crest gives the bird a comical expression. It is a close relative of the brightly coloured turacos (*page 154–155*) but lacks the bright colours of those birds. The Bare-faced Go-away-bird does, however, show a greenish patch on the breast, like a wet grass stain.

Immature birds, often seen being fed by their smaller foster parents, such as this White-browed Robin Chat, are dark-brown above with a white, strongly barred belly.

Juvenile

☐ Red-chested Cuckoo ▶
30 cm 12"
A hawk-like bird with barred underparts. Often referred to as the Rain-bird, these elusive cuckoos are a common feature of the wooded highlands of East Africa on account of their loud, three-note call "*wip-wip-weeu*", which translates to "*it will rain*". Professional meteorologists have nothing to fear, however, as these birds call during the well-known rainy seasons – and quite frequently after the rain has already started! Adults are dark-grey across the upperparts, show a pale-grey head, and have a rich-chestnut band across the chest. Like most African cuckoos, they are brood-parasites, laying their eggs in the active nests of other species, especially the White-browed Robin Chat (*above* and *page 134*) in the Mara.

Adult

Three green gems

A male is shown; female and immature birds are much browner on the back with heavily barred underparts.

Female

Male

Named after the Khoi Khoi servant of French explorer and collector Francois Le Vaillant (1753–1824) who presumably found the bird for him. See Narina Trogon (*page 155*) for more on Le Vaillant's exploits.

◀ ▢ Diederik Cuckoo 19 cm 7½"

A heavily barred cuckoo with a distinctive call. This bird can be found in a variety of habitats, from open woodland to dry acacia scrub. During the wet season, from October to June, you are likely to find it close to the communal hanging nests of the Village Weaver (*page 138*), where the female cuckoo lays her eggs while the weavers are not at home. Superficially similar to the Klaas's Cuckoo, the Diederik Cuckoo is a slightly larger bird with many white spots on the wing and barring on the underparts, including the underwing in flight. The bird's name derives from its loud call, a resonant "*dee-dee-DEE-der-ick*".

▢ Klaas's Cuckoo 18 cm 7"

An emerald cuckoo of woodland and gardens. About the size of a Common Bulbul (*page 124*), this small cuckoo is a brood-parasite of the sunbird family, especially the tiny Collared Sunbird (*page 133*). Males are iridescent green on the head and back and white on the front, whilst females are browner and ◀ heavily barred. Both sexes show a fleck of white behind the eye. In flight, they reveal white outer tail feathers so could be confused with a honeyguide (*page 112*), which shows the same feature. The call is unmistakable, a whistled two-note "*phwee-phuu*", the second note lower than the first, which is often repeated three times.

▢ Little Bee-eater 15 cm 6"

A colourful darting bird of open scrub. As the name suggests, these birds and most of the other species in this family specialize in a diet of bees, wasps and other insects that they catch in flight at breakneck speed. They are often found perched low-down on the edge of bushes, where they wait for their prey to fly by, and call with a series of dry "*chip*" notes. They nest in a burrow in a sandy bank usually, but not always, close to water. The similar Cinnamon-chested Bee-eater (*not shown*) is a larger species preferring highland woods and forests and shows warmer brown tones across the underparts. Also check out the migratory Eurasian Bee-eater on *page 159*. ◀

Striped Kingfisher 17 cm 6¾"

An unobtrusive dowdy kingfisher.
This bird is often found far from
water, where it is a specialist hunter
of grasshoppers and other sizeable
invertebrates. The bill is dark above
and red below – the reverse of
Woodland Kingfisher – and it
shows a dark mask through the eye.
Like the Grey-headed Kingfisher, its
blue colouration is restricted to the
wings and tail. Although shy and
sometimes difficult to find, the Striped
Kingfisher becomes extravert during
its display, when it lands on an exposed
perch, opens it wings, and calls a long,
pulsating "*wi-frreeeeewww*".

Woodland Kingfisher ▶
22 cm 8¾"

A brilliant sky-blue kingfisher
with a red-and-black bill. With its
bright colours, dazzling display
and unforgettable call, this bird
is a favourite among guides and
safari-goers alike. Usually found in
lightly wooded areas, the Woodland
Kingfisher is the bluest of the bush
kingfishers and shows a bright red
upper half to the bill and black
lower half. Like the Striped
Kingfisher, it displays with open
blue wings, and calls a penetrating
"*CHEW-chhrreerrrr*". It will happily
feed on small lizards and amphibians,
as well as invertebrates.

General note: These kingfishers are not
restricted to water and feed primarily
on invertebrates rather than fish. The
colour of the bill, face and back are all
useful identification features and the
calls are distinctive. Their scientific
genus *Halcyon* stems from the mythical
Alcyon bird, which produced 14 days
of calm weather during the northern
winter. Hence, today, Halcyon days are
calm and cloud-free.

■ Grey-headed Kingfisher ▶

21 cm 8¾"

A dark-backed kingfisher with a pale head. Often found in bush and lightly wooded areas, sometimes close to water, this kingfisher shows a chestnut belly below the grey head and breast, whilst the wing-tips and tail are bright blue – most obvious when seen in flight. Its bill is all-red, although young birds may show a dark tip. It is less vocal than the other kingfishers shown here but you may still hear the softly chipped "*tit-tit-tit-tit*" notes that comprise its call.

☐ Common Scimitarbill 30 cm 12″

A black bird with a long tail and
long, decurved bill. Usually found
alone or in pairs, the Scimitarbill
is not as sociable as the similar
Green Wood-hoopoe but frequents
a similar habitat of open woodland.
The very fine bill is strongly curved
along its entire length and is black
– not red as in the wood-hoopoe.
Its feet are also black (not red) and
its plumage lacks any green gloss,
although in excellent light you may
see a purple gloss on the back.
In flight, it is similar to the Green
Wood-hoopoe but shows a narrow
white bar in the wing and lacks the
white spot at the front. It makes a
soft, high-pitched "*sisisisi*" contact
call and a stronger run of downslurred
"*werp-werp-werp*" notes when excited.

▼

◀ ☐ **Green Wood-hoopoe** 37 cm 14½"

A gregarious dark bird with a long tail. Usually found in family groups, the Green Wood-hoopoe appears black on first impression, but good light will reveal an iridescent gloss to the plumage, mostly violet on the wings and tail but green on the head and back. The strong, pointed red bill shows a slight curve and is used to probe tree bark on boughs and trunks for invertebrates. The feet are red. Its long tail is dark with white spots along the outer edge. In flight, the wings show a broad white bar across the flight feathers and a single white spot at the front. They appear quite clumsy as they fly from tree to tree, and stay in contact with chuckling calls.

☐ **Hoopoe** 28 cm 11"

A bright-orange bird with black-and-white stripes in the wing. Unmistakable, with an erectile crest, the Hoopoe can vary in colour from orange to light-brown according to the time of year. It feeds on the ground with a stitching motion, probing the ground with its decurved bill for grubs and worms. On take-off, it shows an elaborate pied decoration of stripes through the rounded wings and tail. It prefers to nest in tree holes but will also nest in stone walls or sandy banks. The call is a low, two-note or three-note series "*poop-poop-poop*" with which guides should be familiar.

Some ornithologists split the Hoopoe into two species – African Hoopoe and Eurasian Hoopoe. The differences are clear to the trained eye but are beyond the scope of this guide.

◀

Male

Immature

◀ ☐ **Greater Honeyguide**
19 cm 7½"

A vocal bird of light, open woodland. You are likely to hear these birds making their repeated, telephone-like, territorial call "*wheet-too*" well before you see them. The first view is usually a good look at their distinctive behinds as they fly off. The flash of white in the outer tail feathers is common to both honeyguides shown here – but be wary of Klaas's Cuckoo (*page 107*) which shares the same feature. The basic plumage of this species is grey below and dull brown above, but the sexes and immature birds can be told apart: males show a black throat and white cheeks; females do not; while immature birds have a bright lemon-yellow wash to the throat and breast and a blue eye-ring.

Both sexes call a soft rattle which lures people and Honey Badgers to bee colonies, where both parties get to enjoy the spoils.

Like cuckoos, honeyguides are brood-parasites, laying their eggs in other birds' nests for the host family to raise. However, honeyguides target different species, specializing in tree-hole nesters such as barbets and woodpeckers.

◀ ☐ Lesser Honeyguide
14 cm 5½"

A shy sparrow-like bird with a dark, stubby bill and grey and olive-green plumage. This is a common resident of wooded areas but can be tricky to find since it often sits still for long periods. Unlike the Greater Honeyguide, it does not attract people or Honey Badgers to bee colonies – but still has a sweet tooth, enjoying beeswax and insects in equal measure – and is happy to feast on the spoils after a bees' nest has been raided by others. The call is a repeated number of "*chip*" notes.

◀ ☐ D'Arnaud's Barbet
19 cm 7½"

A comical yellowish bird with black and white spots. It is common where bush and scrub meet grassy plain, and is often seen sunning itself in the morning light. Barbets are close relatives of woodpeckers but this species tends to be more terrestrial in its habits. The longish tail is heavily barred, while the body is mostly yellowish with black spotting, giving the bird a rather scruffy appearance. Often seen in pairs when they make cyclical, ratchety calls with their tails cocked proudly in the air. The local race of this bird, found only in the Mara-Serengeti ecosystem, is widely known as Usambiro Barbet, and many consider it a distinct species.

113

Female

Male

◀ ☐ Nubian Woodpecker

20 cm 8″

A large, spotted woodpecker of open bush and acacia scrub. A common visitor to old fallen trees on the savannah, this woodpecker shows bold, dark spots on the underparts, pale spots on the upperparts with some fine, pale barring on the wings, and yellow shafts to the tail feathers. Males can be distinguished by their red cap and red 'moustache' (known as the malar stripe), whereas females show a black forehead peppered with white and no 'moustache'. Their flight is heavily undulating. Listen out for the loud call *"keek-keek-kee-kee"*, which gets progressively slower and sounds like a bicycle hurtling downhill while applying bad brakes.

☐ Cardinal Woodpecker ▶

14 cm 5½″

A small, streaked woodpecker of woods and gardens. This woodpecker is very approachable and is frequently found in camps and lodges. A great place to start looking for it is where a collection of animal skulls is exhibited, for they routinely feed on the insect larvae that bury inside the horn of Wildebeest, Eland and Buffalo, to name a few. Unlike the other woodpeckers shown here, the underparts are streaked rather than spotted, and the back and wings show pale barring. The Cardinal in the name derives from the male's red cap; this is not present in female birds.

Like parrots and cuckoos, woodpeckers are zygodactyl, meaning that they have two toes directed forwards and two pointing backwards. Most other birds have one backward and three forward-pointing toes.

Immature male

■ Green-backed Woodpecker
17 cm 6¾″

A medium-sized, spotted woodpecker of woods and gardens. Although superficially similar to the Nubian Woodpecker, both sexes show a speckled throat (this is unmarked in Nubian). Like Nubian, adult males have an all-red crown but lack the red 'moustache'. They are noisy birds, often heard calling "*ker-EEK*" over and over. ▶ ▼

Female

Male

Female

◼ Black-headed Oriole 21 cm 8¼″

A bright-yellow bird of open woodlands. As the name indicates, this bird shows a completely black head, though its bill is bright red. The back can show a hint of green and the central tail feathers are also rich olive-green. The flight feathers are mostly black but edged in white with a small white patch at the base. As with so many woodland birds, getting to know their calls is a great help when trying to locating them – so listen out for the oriole's strong, fluty "*weeeooo*" or descending "*weeo-weeoo*". Two other species of oriole can sometimes be seen in the Mara – Eurasian Golden Oriole and African Golden Oriole – but Black-headed is by far the most commonly encountered and the only one with a black head. ▼

It is always a good idea to ask the best bird guide at your camp or lodge to point out this oriole when they hear it. These are such stunning birds that you will be very glad you did.

◼ Tropical Boubou 21 cm 8¼″ ▶

An easy-to-find bushshrike of open woodland and lodge gardens. At first glance, it appears all-white below and black above, including the eye, with a white bar running across the wing. Given close views, the underparts will be seen to have a peachy flush. There is a chance of confusion with the male Black-backed Puffback (*page 119*), which shares the same habitat – but the puffback is much smaller and has a red eye. As with most bushshrikes, one feature of their behaviour is synchronized calling, known as an antiphonal system. This involves one bird starting the duet with a series of notes and the other bird coming in seamlessly to finish the harmony. Until you see this for yourself, you may find it hard to believe that it is not a single bird making the call, but in fact two. In the case of the Tropical Boubou, "*poo-poo*" by the male is followed immediately by "*wey-hoo*" from the female. You are just as likely to encounter the antiphonal phenomenon with Slate-coloured Boubou (*page 123*) and the puffback.

Like its brighter relative below, the Tropical Boubou is fond of other birds' eggs and nestlings and is frequently seen being harassed or chased by smaller birds within its territory.

■ Grey-headed Bushshrike 25 cm 10"

A stunning bird of wooded areas that hops and glides through the tree canopy in search of a variety of prey, including small reptiles, large insects and, sometimes, young birds. Despite its bright plumage, it can be difficult to locate – so it is well worth familiarizing yourself with its unmistakable call, a drawn-out, mournful whistle "*pheeeeuuuu*", although it can also be heard making a variety of clicking calls and eerie, rising whistles. Generally secretive, every now and again one will put on a great show for you and be seen gliding on spread olive-green wings from one tree or bush to another. If you are this lucky, try to observe how other birds react to it – most will avoid contact with this glamorous but stealthy predator. The similar Sulphur-breasted Bushshrike (*not shown*) is also found in the Mara but is smaller, shows a patch of yellow above the eye leading down to the top of the bill, and sings a sweet, whistled "*phew-pu-pu-pu-puuuuuu*".

Female

Male

☐ Brown-throated Wattle-eye
13 cm 5″

A small, pied bird of woodland and gardens. As their name suggests, both sexes show a distinctive bright-red, fleshy wattle above the eye that contrasts with the otherwise black head. Males show a white throat and black chest-band, while females have a maroon-coloured throat. Both sexes show a white flash in the wing and the back is black (rather than grey, as in the Chin-spot Batis). Wattle-eyes also much prefer thicker woodland. Male birds tend to call first with a low, four-note whistle, translating to "*he likes bam-boo*"; the female replying with a bouncy retort "*she supplies him bam-boo*".

☐ Chin-spot Batis 10 cm 4″

A tiny black, white and grey bird of open woodland and scrub. Both sexes show a grey crown and back, yellow eyes and a broad, white line through the wing. Male birds show a thick black band across the chest, while females have a distinctive rusty-brown spot on the chin (hence the name) and a thinner breast-band of the same colour. If you see one bird of a pair, then the other will be nearby. These attractive birds have a distinctive "*pee....poo*" call, the latter note being much lower than the first, which is often accompanied by snappy and burry notes. Despite their flycatcher-like behaviour, both batises and wattle-eyes are more closely related to shrikes.

Male

Female

☐ Black-backed Puffback

17 cm 6¾"

A heavily marked, black-and-white bushshrike of gardens and open scrub. It is similar in plumage to both the Brown-throated Wattle-eye and Chin-spot Batis, but is much larger and there is only a subtle difference between male and female. Males show a greater contrast between a white belly and black back, while females are browner-backed and greyer below. Both sexes have a red eye. Their name derives from the male's impressive display in which he ruffs up his white rump feathers into a fluffy ball and calls loudly "*took-took-took*", sometimes flying around with his back still puffed-up. Males also emit various whipped "*tikweeoo*" notes.

Displaying male

Female

Male

The family of true shrikes, which includes the two fiscals shown here, are commonly known as 'butcherbirds' on account of their habit of impaling their prey, mostly invertebrates, on thorns and maintaining a 'larder' for harsher times. These are not to be confused with the true butcherbirds that are found in Australia.

■ Grey-backed Fiscal 25 cm 10" ▶

A distinctive long-tailed shrike of open woodland and acacia scrub. The masked appearance of this bird, with grey crown, neck and back, are the best features for separating it from the Common Fiscal. Groups are sociable and engage in fits of tail-wagging while emitting squabbling calls from an exposed perch or sometimes from the ground. In flight, they appear very long-tailed and show a white flash in the wing and outer tail feathers.

Northern White-crowned Shrike
21 cm 8¼"

A gregarious bird of dry scrub and low
bush. Usually encountered in extended
family groups, this distinctive shrike is
very dark-backed and pale-fronted.
The pattern of white crown, dark line
through the eye and black cheeks is
unique among shrikes in the region.
When compared with the fiscal shrikes
shown here, the Northern White-crowned
Shrike is a much stockier bird with a
shorter tail and shows an obvious white
rump in flight. Young birds lack the white
crown and are grubbier-looking. Social
groups are noisy, giving a mix of nasal
and chattering notes, including a Punch
and Judy-like "*weer-haha*".

Common Fiscal 23 cm 9"

A common pied shrike of open
bush, which is by far the most
abundant and widespread of the
shrikes in the Mara. Common
Fiscals are blackish above and
white below with an obvious white
bar across the upperwing when
perched and in flight. The sexes
look similar although females
have a small chestnut patch on the
flanks. It is frequently encountered
perched in the open during game-
drives that pass through bushy
areas. Young birds are browner and
heavily barred. The soft song is a
sad melody of "*twee*" notes.

◀ ☐ Common Drongo
25 cm 10″

A black, fork-tailed bird usually seen perched high in a tree or bush. Often referred to as the Fork-tailed Drongo on account of the deep 'V'-shaped notch in the tail, adult birds have completely glossy blue-black plumage and a red eye. Immature birds are browner with black flecks in the plumage. They are insect hunters and often sit in exposed positions waiting for their quarry to fly by before swooping onto their prey, revealing lighter matt-brown flight feathers that contrast with the black body and tail. They appear more thickset than the slimmer Black Flycatcher, especially around the neck, and show a thicker, slightly hook-tipped bill. The rambling call is a mix of squawks and peeps.

The Slate-coloured Boubou is a vocally versatile bird and, like the Tropical Boubou (*page 116*), has an antiphonal duet calling system. One call starts with a loud "*ch'shh-ch'shh*" followed by a woodblock-sounding "*coco-pop*". Another series starts "*pa-ponk-pa-ponk*" followed by "*wee-eer*" and you might also hear several loud "*queerk-queerk*" notes returned with a low "*donk*".

☐ **Northern Black Flycatcher** ▶
18 cm 7″

A slim, black bird that perches in the middle of trees and bushes. Frequently overlooked by birders and guides, this common matt-black flycatcher lives up to its name when swooping from its perch onto small flying invertebrates. Unlike the Common Drongo, it rarely sits out in the open, preferring to sit midway up a tree or bush with some cover, and is rarely seen on the ground. Young birds (*below right*) are heavily spotted with light-brown dots. It lacks the forked tail and pale flight feathers of the drongo and has dark rather than red eyes. The song is a soft, sweet refrain of quiet whistles and chips but it will sometimes mimic other species.

☐ **Slate-coloured Boubou** 20 cm 8″

A noisy, dark sooty-grey bird of low vegetation in bush and open woodland. This bird can appear all-black but a good view reveals a softer grey plumage especially on the back. Unlike the Common Drongo and Northern Black Flycatcher, this bird spends much of its time hopping on the ground or along low-lying branches and consequently has longer, sturdier legs. It rarely perches high in a tree so this should be a consideration when separating it from the other species shown here. A really useful identification feature for this bird is that the top of the bill obviously cuts upwards into the feathers of the forehead. In the other species shown here, the forehead feathers circle the top of the bill without interruption.

Adult

Juvenile

Getting to know
this bird should
be a priority, as it
is the benchmark
for reference
when describing
the size of many
other songbirds.

◀ ☐ Common Bulbul
18 cm 7″

An abundant brown bird
with a yellow vent. This
is the most widespread of
all East African birds and
there are few places where
it is not found. In the
Mara, you are most likely
to see it in the grounds of
camps and lodges where
it becomes very familiar
and invades food halls and
buffets with regularity.
The common call is a
downward "*he-wee-we-wer*",
often accompanied with
open, quivering wings.

◀ ■ Arrow-marked Babbler
22 cm 8¾"

A medium-sized, dark-brown bird
of bushy areas. This gregarious
species lives in extended family
groups and its noisy scowls leading
into raucous disarray are usually
the first sign of its presence.
The many small, white chevrons
down the throat and chest
account for its name. Adult birds
show bright-yellow eyes, while
those of immatures are darker.
Birds sift through leaf-litter,
tossing it like a salad, looking for
small invertebrates before flying a
short distance on stiff wings to the
next stop.

■ Brown-crowned Tchagra 19 cm 7½"

A secretive, streaky-headed bird of bush
and rank grass. Pronounced "chag-ra", this
small, attractive bushshrike is common
in suitable habitat across the Mara. As an
indicator of habitat suitability, if there are
Rattling Cisticolas (*page 128*) present you
stand a good chance of finding this tchagra.
The rich-chestnut wings help to separate
the Brown-crowned Tchagra from similar
species, such as the Black-backed Puffback
(*page 119*). Its call is a sweet, reverberating,
descending whistle "*TIU-TIU-tiu-tiu-tiu*".
The closely related Black-crowned Tchagra
(*not shown*), is also found in similar habitat
but its head pattern is more striking, with a
whiter face and jet-black crown.

Male

Female

An intricate nest of moss, feathers and spiders' web are fused together between two branches, often near human habitation where the birds feel safe.

African Paradise Flycatcher
36 cm 14"

A stunning chestnut and sooty-grey bird, sometimes with a very long tail. Despite its serene appearance, this is an aggressive, territorial bird that will often chase birds far larger than itself. They catch insects in swooping flights that often involve hovering, before resting on a perch to eat. Males in breeding plumage show an impressive long tail that can be at least three times the length of the head and body combined. Outside the breeding season, the tail streamers are lost and the males then look similar to female and immature birds. The amount of white in the wing depends on the local gene pool; some populations show none at all yet, at the other extreme, some show a high proportion of white. Some birds lack any brown pigment and are completely white – though these are rare in the Mara and you will be very lucky to see one. The sharp contact call "*schwee-shurp*" sounds like the snapping of garden shears.

White-eyed Slaty Flycatcher
15 cm 6"
A blue-grey flycatcher with
prominent white spectacles.
Common within its range, this
flycatcher is most often encountered
in the west of the reserve. It tends
to be less active than the other
flycatchers shown here, usually
sitting quietly on an exposed
perch waiting for prey to fly by
and swooping to catch it in mid-air,
but sometimes feeds by dropping
to the ground. This bird lacks the
bright colouration of the African
Blue Flycatcher and appears a soft
blue-grey all-over with a slightly
paler belly and obvious white
eye-rings. Like the young of the
Northern Black Flycatcher (*page
123*), the young of this species are
heavily spotted with pale feathers
but show the outline of an
emerging white eye-ring. Its call
is an agitated "*chrrrr-chrrrr*".

African Blue Flycatcher
14 cm 5½"
A brilliant ultramarine-blue bird.
Although not numerous in the
Mara, these unmistakable little gems
can sometimes be found along the
riverine woodland at Kichwa Tembo
and Governors' Camp. Look out
for their delightful displays during
which the adult birds raise their
fanned tails and dance with
one another. It sings a
complex rambling
of "*chit-chiti*"
notes.

☐ Rattling Cisticola 14 cm 5½"

The classic 'little brown job' (LBJ) of bush and scrub. This abundant small, brown warbler is heavily streaked above and pale below, with a relatively thick bill. It shows a brown crown that is lightly streaked but this is more chestnut in tone in immature birds. The tail is broad and rudder-like, edged with white spots that are evident in flight. Among the noisiest of small birds, it can often be heard shouting many harsh rasping notes that are followed by the rapid rattle "*chr-chr-chr-chr*".

Approximately 14 species of cisticola have been recorded in the Mara, though only a few show distinctive colouration. They are difficult to identify and only the two commonest are included in this book: the Rattling Cisticola shown here and the Pectoral-patch Cisticola on *page 56*. The species are best separated by habitat preference and their unique calls, many of which are included in their common names, as is the case with Rattling Cisticola. Don't be too hard on yourself if they all look the same – but do concentrate on learning first the ones that you see and hear most often.

Red-faced Crombec 10 cm 4"

A tiny bird with a very short tail. Its
name does not help to describe the
actual colour of this small bird, as
the face and belly are cinnamon or
dark-peach in tone, rather than red.
The crown, back and wings are
greyish-brown, as is the
micro-short tail that may
even appear to be absent.
You will find it climbing
and hopping through bushes
and low trees, one after the
other, in search of food, and may
hear its very high-pitched "*seeu*"
call, although this can be difficult
to trace.

Tawny-flanked Prinia 11 cm 4¼"

A tiny brown bird with a long tail.
Although appearing rather dull at first
glance, the Tawny-flanked Prinia
has a lot of personality for its size.
It is often found in small, active groups
and engage in frantic bouts of
tail-swinging and calling – a zipping
"*cheerp-cheerp*". Birds can be quite
tame at times and a close approach
will enable you to see the red eye and
white eyebrow. The warm-brown
flanks help to separate it from
some other LBJs.

☐ **Grey-capped Warbler** ▲
15 cm 6″
A vocal, green-backed
warbler with a grey crown.
This shy bird is frequently
encountered wherever there
is dark, damp and tangled vegetation,
often near rivers and streams. It will
sing loudly from the undergrowth –
"*wuhu-chit-chit-chit-chit*" – but you
may have to be patient for a bird to
reveal itself. The grey crown contrasts
with a narrow, black face-mask and,
with a very good view, you may see a
small, rusty-coloured bib.

◀ ☐ **Grey-backed Camaroptera** 10 cm 4″
A tiny grey-and-green warbler with a short
tail. You stand a good chance of seeing this
bird wherever there are trees with a rich
understorey of vegetation. The grey head and
back are complemented with moss-green wings.
One feature you may observe when birds are
hopping through the lower branches of dense
vegetation is how white the feathers are under
the tail. Birders will sometimes jest that it is
called the 'camera-operator' because its call is
similar to a camera with a whirring motor-drive
shooting many frames "*di-der-der-der-der-der*".
It can be quite approachable in the gardens of
many of the camps and lodges in the Mara.

▲

☐ **Yellow-breasted Apalis**
13 cm 5″
A long-tailed warbler with a
lemon breast that often shows
a black spot. The head is
bluish-grey and the back and
tail moss-green. A busy little
bird of open bush and scrub,
the Yellow-breasted Apalis is
often found in pairs and has a
unique song – one bird sings a
rising "*ker-ker-keer-keer-keer*",
while the other bird duets
with a galloping horse-like
"*territ-territ-territ*".

131

Scarlet-chested Sunbird 15 cm 6″

A large, dark sunbird of woodland edge and
gardens, with a long, decurved bill. Male birds
have a spectacular red bib that is flecked with
silvery-blue. In very good light, they also show
a green forehead, throat and moustache; the rest
of the bird is black. Females are dark chocolate-
brown with light streaking towards the vent.
Immature males appear similar to females but
are paler and show a hint of the red bib.
Their songis a rapid series of "*chip*" notes.

General note: sunbirds are
small, attractive nectar-feeders
that are always on the go and
often attracted to flowers in
lodge gardens. Males show
bright, iridescent plumage,
while females appear dowdy.
When identifying these birds,
pay particular attention to the
size of the bird, the shape of
its bill and the colour of the
glossy sheen, which changes
according to the light.

Female

Male

Collared Sunbird 10 cm 4″

A tiny, green-and-yellow sunbird. More restricted to woodland and forest than the other sunbirds shown here, the Collared is often seen feeding in trees rather than bushes and its diet includes more invertebrates. The sexes are quite similar – green above and lemon below – but males show an iridescent green breast underlined with a narrow, purple border. The song is less harsh that the other sunbirds – a sweet, piercing "*see-yu*" repeated many times. The tiny nest of this bird is frequently raided by the brood-parasite Klaas's Cuckoo (*page 107*).

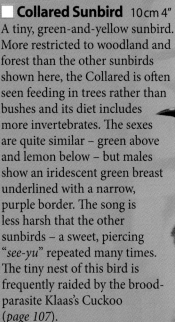

Female

Male

Variable Sunbird

11 cm 4½″

A small sunbird of woodland and dry scrub. Female birds are dull grey-brown above and yellowish-green below, but the variety of colours in the male is a sight to behold. These are very busy birds that barely keep still – which doesn't help when you are trying to identify them! To separate the male from the similar but smaller Collared Sunbird, look for a blue or purple wash across the face and breast. You may also see a small orange feather or two between the wings and the breast – the pectoral tufts. The song is a series of rapid and rising "*chit-chit-chit-chit*" notes.

Male

Female

133

☐ **White-browed Robin Chat** 20 cm 8″

A thrush-sized bird with a grey back and orange underparts. Common in lodge and camp gardens where there are large and scattered trees and lush undergrowth, the White-browed Robin Chat is generally a retiring bird, but can be easily tamed.

With its striking head-pattern, bright underparts and burnt-orange tail in flight, this bird is easily recognised. It is important to be aware that the near-identical Rüppell's Robin Chat (*not shown*), a montane forest species, does not occur in the Mara. The cyclical song starts quietly but increases in volume and pace. Pairs will often engage in powerful duets, especially when rival pairs are nearby, and the noise can be deafening. It is common to see this bird feeding its young, which are similar to the adults but heavily spotted and lack the strong face pattern. If you are very lucky, you may also see adults feeding a dark, heavily barred fledgling that is far larger than itself – this will be a juvenile Red-chested Cuckoo (*page 105*), a species that routinely lays its eggs in robin chat nests.

☐ **Rüppell's Starling** ▶
35 cm 14″

A long-tailed, glossy starling with white eyes. Similar in general appearance to the Greater Blue-eared Starling, the Rüppell's Long-tailed Starling, as it used to be known, shows a long, graduated tail that befits the old name. Its obvious white eyes are set in a matt-black head. The colouration of the body plumage varies among birds of different age and sex.

Most show a deep-purple gloss with a green sheen to the wings, but some birds appear an iridescent cobalt-blue. They are highly vocal birds that sing a continuous, noisy chatter and whining, sometimes in the middle of the night; in flight their wings produce a whooshing sound.

These gaudy blue starlings are typically vocal but if you notice them becoming particularly noisy and agitated, it might be worth investigating further as they frequently harass predators, such as owls and birds of prey. Do proceed with caution, however, as they also mob dangerous snakes!

See under Rüppell's Vulture (*page 37*) to discover more about Rüppell.

▢ **Greater Blue-eared Starling** ▶
23 cm 9″

A large glossy starling with orange-yellow eyes. Although not common, it is widespread in small numbers in the Mara. This green-glossed starling shows a violet-blue sheen around the ears and belly in good light. It can be quite bullish in the company of other birds. The song is a jumbled mix of chittering warbles, but the call is easy to remember if you can imagine an old woman with a whining voice calling her husband Pat in for supper – "*pa-a-at*".

See Hildebrandt's Francolin (*page 95*) to discover more about Hildebrandt.

◀ ◼ Hildebrandt's Starling 19cm 7½"

A colourful, red-eyed starling of open woodland. Very similar in appearance to the Superb Starling, Hildebrandt's is more likely to be encountered in drier, wooded areas. It can be distinguished from Superb Starling by its red, rather than white, eyes and lack of a clean white line between the blue breast and orangey belly. The belly also tends to be more light-peach in colour than the bright orange of Superb Starling. In addition, its back tends to appear much darker blue and this colour extends to the shoulder; in Superb Starling the shoulders are green. In flight, it shows the same peach colour of the belly in the underwing, rather than white. The song comprises a series of slow-paced "*woo-wah*" notes mixed with chattering.

Adult

Juvenile

Look out for their nests in the tangle of old desert palm trees, often referred to as Balanites.

Young Superb Starling can be separated from Hildebrandt's of the same age by their dark breast and white vent.

▢ Violet-backed Starling 17 cm 6¾"

A small starling of open bush and woodland.
Unlike the other starlings in this guide,
the sexes of this species are very different.
Males show white underparts and a brilliant,
iridescent, violet-coloured back, which
accounts for its other names – Amethyst
or Plum-coloured Starling. It sings a series
of quickly trilled notes. Females are light-
brown above and pale below but show dark
streaking throughout. Flocks of these
birds move with the seasons and the
fruiting of trees, but often return
to the same areas to breed in
tree holes. In poor light, be
careful as the glossy
male can appear to
be just black-
and-white.

▶

Male

◀ ▢ Superb Starling 19 cm 7½"

A common, multicoloured bird
of open bush and plains. Often
encountered in family groups,
the Superb Starling lives up to
its name with its 'coat of many
colours'. When separating adults
from the similar Hildebrandt's
Starling, look for the
obvious white line
that divides the blue
breast from the orange
underparts, and the white
eyes in its black face. In flight
it shows white under the wing
and often calls a cheerful
"cheera-cherr-eet".

Female

137

Male

Female

◀ ☐ Spectacled Weaver 14 cm 5½″

An orange-faced, yellow weaver with pale-eyes. Often encountered in well-wooded areas, this unobtrusive weaver is aptly named on account of its narrow, black eye-mask. The face of both sexes has a warm glow and males also possess a black throat. Like the Baglafecht, this weaver has a pointed, slender bill but shows a plain moss-green coloured back. The call is often the first sign of its presence – a rapid, high-pitched, downward run of "*pipipipi*" notes

☐ Baglafecht Weaver 15 cm 6″

▼ A pale-eyed weaver with black neck and cheeks. This distinctive bird is often found in pairs or small family groups. Males have black cheeks, neck and back, with fine, yellow lines down the wings and tail. The similar females show an all-black crown and face. The bill is black, slender and pointed and the call is a buzzing, downward trill.

Male

▼ ☐ Village Weaver 17 cm 6¾″

A large, stout-billed, gregarious weaver with a red eye. Large colonies can often be found in acacia trees overhanging water. Breeding males are best identified by their black face that extends above the forehead, and the heavy, black stripes running down the back. Females and non-breeding males lack the black face and heavy streaking on the back, instead showing greyish backs and a yellow throat and breast. The belly can be either white, or yellow. The call comprises a series of repeated dry "*chip*" notes, while the song is a heady mix of wheezing and electronic-sounding "*whee*" notes. The most similar species is the Vitelline Masked Weaver of acacia country (*page 149*), but that bird is smaller and the breeding male lacks the black tramlines down the back.

Male

138

Baglafecht Weavers do not nest in colonies and the untidy nest is often attached directly to a main branch rather than dangling down as in Village Weaver.

The woven nest of the **Village Weaver** hangs from a long 'stalk' and has an obvious bulbous chamber.

The nest of the **Spectacled Weaver** is very distinctive, having a long, tube-like entrance hanging from the side of the main chamber.

Spectacled Weaver
Juvenile

Baglafecht Weaver
Female

Village Weaver
Female

General note: Weavers are a large family of sparrow-sized birds that show great variation in their plumage. Most show varying amounts of yellow, with black in the face and body plumage. When identifying species, look out for the following features: face pattern; eye colour; bill size and shape; extent of markings on the back; nest shape; and social behaviour (*i.e.* is it in a flock?).

139

◄ ☐ **Purple Grenadier**

13 cm 5″

A stunning purple -and-brown waxbill. Widespread in dry bush and scrub though rarely seen in numbers, this beautiful little bird shows a brown back, violet-blue rump and dark tail in both sexes. Males have patchy purple areas in the breast and belly, while females show brown bars below. Both sexes have decorative colouration around the eyes – dark-blue in males but light-blue and studded in females. It is often found feeding near the base of bushes and thickets, giving a soft, high-pitched call "*tseet-tseet*" as it moves around – a sound you may struggle to hear.

Male

The three species shown here belong to the waxbill or Estrildid family. Although they do not possess 'waxbill' in their common names, they are related to the Common Waxbill on *page 91*.

Female

Bronze Mannikin 9 cm 3½"

A tiny, brown waxbill with a white belly. Often occurring in small numbers in well-wooded areas and gardens, these birds also gather in flocks to feed on grass seeds at the woodland edge. The mostly dark-brown plumage shows barring on the flanks, while the shoulders have a dark green gloss in good light. The bill is short and stout, typical of granivorous (seed-eating) birds. It is most frequently heard in flight, when the short, buzzing "*pee-pu*" call catches the attention. ▼

Red-cheeked Cordon-bleu
13 cm 5"

A delicate waxbill with bright blue underparts and light-brown back. Frequent in open bush, gardens and lightly wooded areas, you may also see them in villages, often in pairs, mixing with the Red-billed Firefinch (*page 152*). The common call, a high-pitched "*peet-pit-pit-pit*", is quite similar to that of the firefinch. The sexes look similar, both having pinkish bills and brown crowns, but females lack the dark-red cheek-patch of the male. They are a common host to the Pin-tailed Whydah (*page 143*), a brood-parasite of the waxbill family. ▼▼

Female

Male

141

Yellow-fronted Canary
11 cm 4¼"

A yellow finch with a greenish, streaked back. This canary shows an all-yellow belly and dark-green stripes on the face. It is often found along woodland edges and in grassland with scattered bushes, unlike the similar White-bellied Canary (*page 147*) that is generally found in drier areas, especially where acacia scrub abounds. However, beware, for the bright-yellow breast and eyebrow is common to both species. These close relatives will sometimes mix where habitats meet, so pay close attention to belly colour. Both canaries gather in small groups and show bright yellow rumps as they take off.

Golden-breasted Bunting 15 cm 6"

An attractive bird with a golden-yellow breast and a striped head. These birds are widespread in the Mara where there is open woodland and scrub. They are shy and often take flight when disturbed from the ground (where they feed), but often just into a nearby tree or bush allowing close inspection. Given good views you will see a mix of black and white stripes on the head and two white bars in the wings. The mostly yellow breast has an orange hue that shines like gold in good light. They are most often encountered in pairs, never in flocks, and males sing their twittering song from an exposed perch high in a tree – a delightful "*tee-tu-tee-tu*" ending with a pronounced "*pee-chew*".

142

Display flight

◼ **Pin-tailed Whydah** 31 cm 12″
Small, seed-eating birds with a variety
of plumages. Breeding males display
impressive long tail streamers which they
dangle in a hanging flight over the drab
brown females while calling continuously
"*tsweet-tsweet-tsweet*". Non-breeding males
look similar to the stripe-headed females
but still retain a red bill and have more
white in the face. They are closely related
to the Village Indigobird (*page 152*) and,
like that species, are a brood-parasite of the
waxbill family. However, unlike cuckoos
and many other brood-parasites, whydahs
and indigobirds do not evict the eggs of the
host family and their chicks grow up with
the rest of the brood.

Male

Female

143

◀ ☐ Blue-naped Mousebird
35 cm 14"

A small grey bird with a long tail. Very similar in size and shape to the Speckled Mousebird (*page 102*), the Blue-naped prefers much drier, open habitats and is particularly fond of acacia. Its plumage is mostly grey, rather than brown as in Speckled, the cheeks are plain (rather than white), and it has a red eye-patch extending to the base of the bill. It also shows a more pronounced, stiff crest which adds to its elegant appearance. Listen out for the distinctive high-pitched "*peeu-peeu-peeu*" call when in flight, which is rapid and direct rather than clumsy and weak as in Speckled.

☐ Abyssinian Scimitarbill
24 cm 9½"

A slender black bird with a long, strongly decurved bill, which is orange in adults and dark in young birds. Very similar in appearance to the Common Scimitarbill (*page 110*), the Abyssinian prefers much drier, open habitats, especially acacia scrub. A diagnostic feature is the lack of any white bars or spots in the wings and tail – obvious during its floppy flight. In good light, look for a violet sheen to the upperparts of this bird. It is often seen hanging on small tree trunks ▶ and branches probing for invertebrates. Listen for its descending "*kree-kree-kree*" call.

Female

Male

☐ Von der Decken's Hornbill

48 cm 19"

A black-backed hornbill with a red or black bill. These birds are slow-moving and rather clumsy inhabitants of acacia thicket, where they feed on a variety of fruits, invertebrates and small reptiles. Males show a bright red bill with a yellow tip, while the females' is black. Unlike other small hornbills found in Kenya, this bird shows an unspotted back in both sexes and two large white wing-panels, most obvious during its undulating flight. Its call is a low, unassuming "*kuk-kuk-kuk-kuk*". Like the African Grey Hornbill (*page 102*), this species seals the entrance to the nest hole to deter predators and nest-site rivals, the imprisoned female incubating the eggs and raising the young while being fed through a small opening by the male.

▲

Named after Baron Carl Claus von der Decken (1833–1865), a German explorer who was the first European to attempt a Kilimanjaro summit climb. He failed.

☐ African Grey Flycatcher

14 cm 5½″

A small, grey bird with a lightly streaked crown. It shows a rather large head for its body size, the black eye on the plain face giving it a rather 'beady-eyed' appearance. Often found sitting upright on the outer branches of an acacia or other small bush in the dry belt, this rather plain flycatcher is usually found in small, loose parties. Rather than taking flies on the wing, as with the African Paradise Flycatcher (*page 126*), this bird generally drops to the ground for its quarry. You are more likely to hear its "*shree-shree*" alarm call than its simple song.

◻ Silverbird 18 cm 7"

An attractive silver-grey
flycatcher with orange
underparts. The distinctive
plumage makes the adults
unmistakable given a
good view, but immature
birds are more difficult to
identify, as they are brown
and lightly spotted with buff
and black. It is likely to be
encountered only in open
acacia scrub in the north
and east of the reserve,
where pairs are common.
Like many flycatchers, it
sits and waits for its prey
to fly by. They are shy and
as they rarely allow a close
approach you are unlikely
to hear the sweet whistled
"*cheet-siri-EET-weet*" song.

◻ White-bellied Canary
11 cm 4½"

A yellow, lightly streaked
finch with a white belly.
Very similar to the Yellow-
fronted Canary (*page 142*),
the White-bellied prefers
drier country with acacia
scrub, although sometimes
the species mingle where
habitats meet. It is a seed-eater
that feeds mostly on the ground
and always shows a white belly
and less heavy facial streaking
than the Yellow-fronted. It is
not shy and is often present
around Maasai people in
and around their villages.

The nest is an untidy bundle of dry grasses often on the outermost branches of a Whistling Thorn acacia, and sometimes showing a prominent entrance hole. Occasionally, pairs will combine nests making a double- or even treble-sized nest that is shared.

◀ ☐ Grey-capped Social Weaver   11 cm 4½"

A very small, brown weaver likely to found in large colonies in the dry lands. A busy colony may exceed 100 birds and you are likely to find them by hearing their busy calls, a series of "*chew chew-chew*" notes. Obvious identification features include the creamy-grey cap and the very short tail that has a whitish tip. Note that the plumage is quite unlike any of the other weavers or sparrows in the Mara.

▼ ☐ Speckle-fronted Weaver
11 cm 4½"

A small, sparrow-like weaver that is common in barren areas of acacia scrub and also sometimes around the outskirts of villages. It is best identified by the chestnut-brown patch at the back of the neck, but also look for the speckled forehead, although this can often be difficult to see. It has a pale face and appears rather beady-eyed, setting it apart from other small birds in the same flock. The nest tends to be more hidden than those of most other weavers, often to be found low down in an acacia rather than hanging from the end of a branch.

Check out the similar sparrows on *page 150*.

The nest of the Vitelline Masked Weaver is very easy to identify as it is always onion-shaped and rarely shows an entrance tube.

Male

Female

◀ ☐ Vitelline Masked Weaver 13 cm 5″

A common weaver that is at home in and around villages in the dry acacia belt. It is similar to the larger Village Weaver (*page 138*) but can be easily separated given a good view. Although both species have red eyes and a warm-chestnut border to their black face-mask, the black on the male Vitelline's head does not extend onto the crown or down onto the breast, and its back does not have strong black 'tramlines' as in Village Weaver. The female Vitelline shows a pale, narrow bill compared to the dark, heavy bill of the female Village Weaver, and the breast and flanks are generally a warm buff contrasting with a white belly.

Check out the similar weavers on *page 138*.

The technical term for seed-eating birds is granivorous.

☐ Grey-headed Sparrow
15 cm 6″

The common grey-headed sparrow in the Mara. This local race of the variable Grey-headed Sparrow "super-species" is known as Swahili Sparrow, has the smallest bill of the group and may well be a species in its own right. This is a gentle-looking sparrow that, like the other sparrows shown here, is very much at home in the company of people, feeding primarily on the ground. Its calls are quite unmusical, mostly dry "*chips*" and not much else. The white bar in the wing is not always easy to see.

☐ Kenya Rufous Sparrow
14 cm 5½″

The native equivalent of the House Sparrow that is common in and around villages, but also around large hotels and tented camps, especially in the east of the Mara. Both sexes can easily be told from House Sparrow by their white eyes, and males show grey rather than white cheeks. Although females lack the 'sparkle' of the males, they are still more colourful than female House Sparrows and often show chestnut on the back and warm tones to the face.

Male

Female

The nests of all three species shown here are generally more secluded than in the closely related weavers, often being built in the thatched roof of a building or a tree hole.

☐ House Sparrow 14 cm 5½"

A common species that will probably be familiar to visitors from most parts of the world. The House Sparrow was introduced to the coast of East Africa around 100 years ago but has spread to the Mara and beyond and is now a regular in Maasai bomas and villages. Males show a distinctive head-pattern: white cheeks; a large, black throat-patch bleeding into the top of the breast; a grey crown; and dark-chestnut at the back of the neck. Females are very bland, lacking much in the way of colour. Both sexes have dark eyes, unlike the Kenya Rufous Sparrow, adults of which have white eyes. House Sparrows give a classic, monotonous chirping call.

Male

Female

The House Sparrow is one of the most successful bird species in the world and occurs on all continents apart from Antarctica. Although it is an introduced species in East Africa, it is quite passive and does not appear to pose a threat to other native species.

Male

Female

Male

Female

Red-billed Firefinch 10 cm 4″

A tiny, red-and-brown waxbill. These are common ground-feeders that associate with sparrows and doves in villages and towns, often in flocks of 20 or more, but may also be found in leafy gardens. Males are deep-red, like a fine claret, with a red-and-grey bill. The back is brown and you may be able to see many tiny white dots around the breast area. Females are light-medium brown all-over, with a distinctive red rump, and typically show brighter white spots on the underparts than males. This firefinch frequently associates with the Village Indigobird that is a brood-parasite dependent upon this species. The rarely encountered African Firefinch (*not shown*) is similar, but birds of both sexes show a black vent and a silver-blue bill.

Village Indigobird 10 cm 4″

A tiny black bird with a white bill and pink legs. Usually found in close association with the Red-billed Firefinch, male indigobirds are easy to pick out in the crowd. Females are slightly trickier due to their drab brown plumage but can be separated from the very similar female Pin-tailed Whydah (*page 143*) by their plain breast lacking any stripes. Village Indigobirds are part of the whydah family which are brood-parasites and specialize in laying their eggs in the nests of Red-billed Firefinch. Strangely, the host does not seem to mind sharing its home with the indigobird and the young grow up with a healthy bond.

Pied Crow 46 cm 18″

A large, black bird with a white breast and neck. Like many other crows around the world, this is a clever opportunist that forages around towns and villages in search of food. It will often steal food from other birds and animals, and may then store the bounty for leaner times. The larger, but otherwise similar, White-necked Raven (*not shown*) is sometimes seen in the Mara but can easily be separated from the Pied Crow at a distance by its black breast and smaller white patch at the back of the neck. A close view will reveal the raven's far thicker bill. The gruff "*caar-caar*" notes are typically crow-like.

Crows are capable of complex problem-solving and one of the few bird families that have a proven ability to count.

☐ Schalow's Turaco 40 cm 16"

Secretive but brightly plumaged birds of
tall riverine woodland and open forests.
Given the incredible colouration of these
birds, it is perhaps a surprise that they are
usually heard before they are seen. The call
is a series of up to ten raucous "*caw*" notes
that rises in volume and intensity for the
first five notes before subsiding.
This is usually repeated every thirty
seconds or so. The first glimpse of this ▶
bird is usually as it glides from one
tree to the next on bright-red wings
that contrast with the bright-green
body and blue tail. A close view of
the face reveals even more beauty
– a red ring around the eye with
a short, white line in front and a
longer white line below; and a
long, green crest with each
feather tipped in white.

The green colour in the
turaco's plumage comes
from the pigment
turacoverdin, and the red
colour in the wings from
the pigment turacin, both
of which are unique among
turaco species. In other birds,
these colours are produced
from carotenoids.

Male

Female

> This bird was named in honour of
> the explorer Levaillant's Khoi Khoi
> girlfriend whose local name he could
> not pronounce. Instead he gave
> her the name Narina, which means
> 'flower' in her native language.

◀ ☐ Ross's Turaco 54 cm 21″

A large, purple bird of the forest with a
distinctive yellow face and bill. Although
closely related to Schalow's Turaco, Ross's
Turaco does not show any green in the
plumage and appears a vibrant purple in
good light. It shares the bright-red flight
feathers, which are most easily seen as
the bird glides through the tree canopy.
Close views will also reveal a red crest.
Immature birds are similar but lack
the yellow face and bill. These birds
are reluctant fliers but are very adept
at running and hopping through the
tree canopy. It is most likely to be
encountered at Kichwa Tembo camp
and the riverine forest of the upper Mara
River, sometimes forming small groups.
The call is a growled "*ko-kow-kow*".

☐ Narina Trogon 30 cm 12″

An elusive bird of the forest
that sits still for long periods.
Although brightly coloured,
like the turaco species, trogons
can be rather difficult to locate
in the wooded areas where
they occur but they can be very
relaxed around people and a
good local guide should be able
to find them for you. Look out
for the bright splash of colour as
birds make short flights to catch
invertebrates from branches
and leaves before returning
to a perch. Males are brighter
than females and both sexes
show white under the tail. The
call is distinctive – a repeated
mournful "*kroo-KROOO*"
with a strong emphasis on
the second note.

Grey-throated Barbet 18 cm 7″

A solid, plain-looking bird with pale eyes and tufts above the bill. At certain times of year, these birds can be seen gorging themselves on fruit, especially figs, at camps and lodges where tracts of rich forest remain, especially Kichwa Tembo. They prefer to arrive at first light to feast on the fruits before small primates, such as the Copper-tailed Monkey, take over, causing the barbets to disperse into the forest. It is a chunky-looking barbet with very unusual bristle feathers above the bill that stand out like horns. Knowing the call – a high "*kweee*" – can help in locating these birds, but also listen out for some social chattering when groups converge.

Double-toothed Barbet 20 cm 8″

A brightly coloured barbet with a large horn-coloured bill. This stunning barbet is another fruit eater that is very fond of figs, amongst others. As with the Grey-throated Barbet, your best chance of seeing it is early in the morning when they attend fruiting trees before primates arrive. A good view of the bright, horn-coloured bill reveals a double ridge, like two teeth, and many long, black bristles at the base. The bright-red face and underparts are very distinctive. When birds have their backs towards you, look out for the bright-white rump, which is conspicuous in the dark foliage. The most common call is a short, sharp "*kwerk*".

☐ Black-and-white Casqued Hornbill 68 cm 27″

A large, black-and-white forest hornbill. These spectacular birds are usually found in loose family parties feeding on fruiting trees where there is good forest cover. They conduct circuits of their territory, visiting their favourite trees, which they will sometimes defend against marauding monkeys. Males show a distinctive raised protrusion, known as a casque, on top of the heavy bill, while females have a much smaller bill and casque. Both birds show extensive white in the wings and tail in flight. They are frequently heard before they are seen, so listen out for the loud, far-carrying bray "*waaah-wah-ah-ah-aaaaaah*", akin to a baby wailing, which can carry for several kilometres.

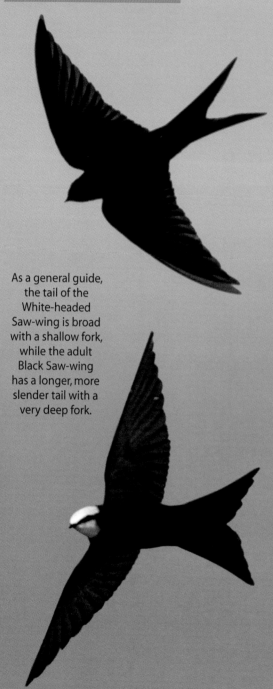

Black Saw-wing 15 cm 6"
An all-black swallow with a forked tail. Seen well in good light, it obviously lacks the white head of the White-headed Saw-wing, but is otherwise very similar. The best identification feature is the long tail which shows a very deep fork. The plumage is blacker than the dark chocolate-brown of White-headed Saw-wing, although this can be difficult to determine when birds are flying and appear in silhouette. The Black Saw-wing is rarely found away from forest, and is most often seen along the Mara River and in the forest at Kichwa Tembo and the Sabaringo Valley.

As a general guide, the tail of the White-headed Saw-wing is broad with a shallow fork, while the adult Black Saw-wing has a longer, more slender tail with a very deep fork.

White-headed Saw-wing
14 cm 5½"
A smart, dark-brown swallow with a white head. These delightful little birds breed in the sandy banks of rivers usually where there is a tangle of tree roots to conceal the nest hole. Although they are most frequently found along the edges of riverine forest, they are sometimes seen over the open plains. Adult males have a crisp, white cap and chin making them very distinctive, while females typically only show a pale chin. Immatures lack the white head markings and are almost impossible to separate from immature Black Saw-wings. Both saw-wing species give a simple, drawn-out "*chew*" call with some random chattering.

Eurasian Bee-eater 28 cm 11″

A stunning migrant from Europe that is often seen migrating overhead in sizeable flocks. Birds typically appear on their southward journey between the end of September and early November, and then again heading north in March and April, although small numbers are suspected to spend their winter in the Mara. Listen for their soft, churring "*prruut-prruut*" calls as they drift leisurely overhead, and enjoy watching them make dashing flights after bees, wasps and dragonflies. This is one of the few examples where the European member of a family is arguably more attractive than its African counterparts, such as the common, resident Little Bee-eater (*page 107*).

☐ Barn Swallow 19 cm 7½"

A blue swallow with a red throat and pale belly. Familiar to many visitors from outside of Kenya, the Barn Swallow is among the most cosmopolitan of all bird species. It is a common migrant to the Mara between September and April, but stragglers have been recorded in all months of the year. In flight, it appears glossy-blue above and cream-coloured on the belly. When perched, good views of the velvet-red throat and blue breast-band help to separate it from the Angola Swallow (*not shown*), which is a less frequent visitor to the Mara. That species shows a reddish-orange throat, light dusky-grey underparts, and lacks the blue breast-band. Young Barn Swallows are less strongly marked than adults and lack the long tail streamers of birds in breeding plumage (as do many adults that arrive into Kenya from September onwards).

☐ Wire-tailed Swallow 18 cm 7"

A blue swallow with a chestnut cap and white underparts. This is a widespread resident of the Mara occurring almost everywhere. It frequently breeds close to water, including under bridges, and may also be found nesting in outbuildings, especially at airstrips. The end of the tail is straight and, in most plumages, shows two prominent stiff and straight outer tail feathers. By far the best identification feature is the clean white throat and belly, which separates it from other blue-backed swallows.

■ Plain Martin 12 cm 4¾"

A brown martin of riverine habitats. Also known as the Brown-throated or African Sand Martin, this bird is very common along the rivers of the Mara reserve. It is mostly sandy-brown all over but has a whitish belly and a dark, grey-brown throat. It excavates nest holes in sandy river banks, and colonies of this bird are easily observed along the Mara River but less so along the Talek River. Other bird species, including swifts, swallows and other martins, frequently take over the nest holes. Two other brown martins occur in the Mara: the Sand Martin, which is a long-distance migrant from Europe and Asia; and the larger Banded Martin, which is a short-distance migrant from other areas in East Africa (*neither are shown*). Both show a white throat and dark-brown band across the chest.

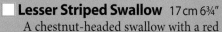

■ Lesser Striped Swallow 17 cm 6¾"

A chestnut-headed swallow with a red rump and heavily striped underparts. It is a common resident with a preference for riverine habitats, where it frequently nests under bridges. These attractive birds will also nest in camps and lodges wherever an overhang provides shelter, such as under the fly-sheets of tents or the eaves of lodge roofs. Although not as common, three other 'red-rumped', blue-backed swallows also occur in the Mara: the large Mosque Swallow (which has white under the wing and pale cheeks); the scarce Rufous-chested Swallow (which has blue cheeks and warm, red underparts); and the migrant Red-rumped Swallow (which shows a black vent) (*none are shown*). These species all have blue caps.

Little Swift 14 cm 5½"

One of two common swifts in the
Mara that show a white rump and
white throat. The Little Swift is best
separated from the White-rumped
Swift by its very short, square-ended
tail. It is very common around villages
where it often forms large, chittering
flocks overhead. Birds range widely
across plains to feed and are often
seen over rivers and marshes.
It regularly breeds in solid
buildings and makes its nest
from feathers and its own
saliva. During display, this
swift will often find a feather
and fly with it in its bill as an
invitation to others that it
is ready to mate.

White-rumped Swift 15 cm 6"

The other common swift with a white
rump that is regularly seen over the
villages, plains and marshes of the Mara.
It is separated from the Little Swift by
its much longer, forked tail, although in
level flight the fork is not always visible
and the tail looks long and pointed.
To be sure of your identification, just
wait a while until it banks and spreads
its tail. Another feature to look out for is
a thin white line along the rear edge of
the upperwing – known as the
'trailing edge' – which is lacking in
Little Swift. As in that species, and
given a close view, you may also notice a
clean white throat on this bird. White-
rumped Swifts will often breed under
bridges, with or without water running
underneath, and may make some
excited trilling sounds as they return to
the nest.

☐ African Palm Swift 18 cm 7"

A uniform, light-brown swift with a long, pointed tail. As its name suggests, this resident species is dependent upon palm trees for nesting and it can often be found hawking for insects in their vicinity. It is common at Keekorok Lodge in the south of the reserve and wherever palms are abundant. The long tail often appears fused at the tip but when banking in the air, it is frequently opened to reveal a deep notch.

☐ Nyanza Swift 17 cm 6¾"

A dark-brown swift with pale wing-panels. This species appears very similar to the Common Swift but in the fast, active flight, the pale patches on the wings can usually be seen – both from above and below.
It is worth noting, however, that the Nyanza Swift is resident in Kenya (breeding mostly in the Rift Valley), and so can be seen year-around in the Mara (and not just between October and April as with Common Swift). It is often seem singly or in small numbers rather than vast flocks. Its call is a trill rather than a scream, but birds tend not to be very vocal in the Mara.

☐ Common Swift 18 cm 7"

A dark-brown swift with a lightly forked tail.
A common migrant from Europe and Asia between October and April, the Common (or Eurasian) Swift often arrives ahead of big storms and in huge numbers. Loose flocks can number in excess of 10,000 birds and may take hours to pass overhead – a great example of bird migration that you can actually sit back, admire and enjoy! Like other swifts, they fly very quickly, so getting a good view requires some dexterity with your binoculars. They are generally silent when wintering in Africa, but if you are from Europe or Asia, you may be familiar with their high-pitched screams that herald the arrival of the northern summer.

Pearl-spotted Owlet 19 cm 7½"

A tiny, spotted owl of open scrub and wooded savannah. Despite its small size, not much bigger than a sparrow, this fearsome little predator regularly takes small birds and sometimes small mammals, reptiles and large invertebrates. It is primarily nocturnal but can also be active during the day. The large, bright-yellow eyes glare and you may also notice the neat pair of white eyebrows. On the back of the head is a pair of black 'false eyes' which may intimidate predators. The chest is streaked with chestnut-brown and the bird gets its name from the numerous small, creamy spots on its back. The commonest call is a continuous piped "*peu-peu-peu*" that rises to a crescendo and finishes with long whistles. This is a useful call to learn, since many small birds are attracted to it and will mob the dangerous owl.

Slender-tailed Nightjar 25 cm 10"

An amazingly camouflaged nocturnal bird of open acacia areas. A good local guide may know where to find one roosting on the ground during the day. They become easier to see as they rise to hawk for insects at dusk and dawn, sometimes coming to feed on moths at the lights of lodges and camps, when it looks like a falcon or a large swift. This is the most abundant of the nine species of nightjar resident in the Mara, and hence is the one you are most likely to encounter. At night, listen out for its monotonous call which is similar to a car alarm "*we-we-we-we-we…*"; in flight, its call is a squeaky "*wik-wik-ik*". ▼

Verreaux's Eagle Owl 66 cm 26"

A huge owl of bush and open woodland. This is the largest owl in Africa and the third largest owl species in the world. It is very powerful and capable of killing prey such as small antelope, small cats and large snakes. They are highly territorial birds and adult males may fight to the death. Birds are occasionally encountered at night at some camps and lodges, as well as on night-drives in the conservancies. However, they are more often seen perched in open trees at first light or at sunset, when their distinctive silhouette stands out clearly. In the middle of the day, they will generally roost out of sight in a large tree. The deep, booming "*hoo-hoooo*" call is not dissimilar to that of the Southern Ground Hornbill (*page 35*) and sometimes these birds are attracted to the calling owls. Young birds often call a painful, drawn-out "*eee-errrr*" that is repeated over and over.

Named after the French bird specimen collector J. P. Verreaux (1807–1873)

References and useful resources

References

The Birds of East Africa by John Fanshawe and Terry Stevenson
The Birds of Kenya and Northern Tanzania by Dale Zimmerman, Don Turner and David Pearson
I highly recommend both of these outstanding books to anyone interested in taking their birding to the next level and for East African explorations beyond the Masai Mara.

Whose Bird? by Bo Beolens and Michael Watkins
The anecdotes about the people that have birds named after them were gleaned from this book. It is a highly interesting read that I cannot recommend highly enough.

Birds of Africa – South of the Sahara by Ian Sinclair and Peter Ryan
The most comprehensive field guide to the birds of this incredible continent.

Highly recommended viewing

The Life of Birds by Sir David Attenborough (BBC)

Online resources

www.maasaimara.com
For unbiased, informative, accurate and up to date information on all things relating to the Masai Mara National Reserve. The expert team also produces a must-have tourist guide book which is available at most camps and lodges in and around the reserve.

www.naturekenya.org
The very friendly and professional team is always there to assist in any matter relating to the wildlife of Kenya and I highly recommend joining the organisation.

www.surfbirds.com
A great website with up-to-date bird news from around the world. It is also a great place to showcase the bird images from your safari.

www.disabledbirdersassociation.co.uk
A fantastic resource that seeks to improve access for people with disabilities to reserves, facilities and services for birding.

www.fatbirder.com
You don't have to be overweight to enjoy this web resource about birds, birding and birdwatching for birders.

Acknowledgements

Such a book would not be possible without the help of many people – so I would like to take this opportunity to thank those who have given me generous assistance along the journey, or *safari*.

First and foremost, I would like thank my wife Vicki for so many things: for bringing me to Africa, indulging my bird obsession, taking on the lion's share of office work and giving me the time to write, proofing the text, allowing me to use some of her wonderful images… The list is endless actually but, most of all, thanks for being my wife and looking out for me.

To the outstanding safari guides of Naibor Camp, past and present; David Mpoe, Daudi Lolotuno, Peter "Lolo" Lolotuno, Mathew Lalaigwanani, Nelson Kirrokorr, Petro Naurori and David Mpusia. I hope you guys find this guide useful as it was originally designed just for you. Keep up the excellent work and maintain your impeccable professionalism. You have all been, and continue to be, a huge credit to Naibor, your people and to Kenya. I salute you!

To the Directors of Naibor Camp - Nigel Archer, Satyan Patel and Anthony Cheffings; thanks for your unwavering support during our tenure as managers of your fabulous camp in the Masai Mara. I hope we've done you proud gentlemen.

To Tony and Betty Archer; many thanks for your huge support behind this book and for the generosity and kindness you have shown to Vicki and I since we arrived in Kenya. You still make the best G&T in Kenya!

For their generosity in providing accommodations, fabulous hosting and friendship and support; the entire &Beyond team at Kichwa Tembo/ Bateleur Camp led superbly by Niall Anderson (you guys ROCK!), Rekero Camp (Jackson, Jono, Dudu and Gerard), Alex Walker's Serian Camp, Patrick and Karen Plumbe, Johann du Toit, the friendly team at Sala's Camp led by Sissa Faull, and our good friend Mike Cheffings (Bateleur Safaris), without whom we may not have arrived in Kenya in the first place!

An educated understanding of the birdlife of the Masai Mara is simply not possible without consultation with Brian Finch who is, to my mind, the most dedicated and knowledgeable birder in East Africa today. I thank you Brian for your kindness and assistance with those various lists and accurate reports. You have helped me, above all others, in developing my own understanding of the birds inhabiting this amazing place.

To Ian Pendleton; thanks for giving me the confidence to actually write a book. You said it could only be done with great organisation and proper planning - but I did it anyway!

Finally to the team at **Wild**Guides: Rob Still, Andy Swash & Brian Clews. Massive thanks for making this book so beautiful and for sharing my aspirations. Shall we do some more?

Photographic credits

Scientific names of the bird species included in this book

The following list gives the scientific names of the bird species covered in this book and uses the names adopted by the Bird Committee of Nature Kenya. English names are highlighted in **bold** for those species that are illustrated. The page number for the main account for each species is included for ease of reference. The other species mentioned in the book that are not illustrated are shown in normal text.

Index

Names in **bold** highlight the species that are afforded a full account.
Bold numbers indicate the page number of the main species account.
Bold blue numbers relate to other page(s) on which a photograph appears.
Normal black numbers are used to indicate the page(s) where the species is mentioned,
but not illustrated. For scientific names, see *page 168*.